Albert Gold

Our Philadelphia: A Candid and Colorful Portrait of a Great City

Other Books by Frank Brookhouser

SHORT STORIES

Request for Sherwood Anderson (1947)
She Made the Big Town (1952)

NOVEL

Now I Lay Me Down (1955)

OUR PHILADELPHIA

A Candid and Colorful Portrait of a Great City

by Frank Brookhouser

Drawings by Albert Gold

DOUBLEDAY & COMPANY, INC., GARDEN CITY, NEW YORK
1957

Library of Congress Catalog Card Number: 57-12461

Printed in the United States of America
First Edition

This Book Is for—

Helen
and my Mother and Dad
and my newspaper friends
and, someday, little K.B.K.

Acknowledgments

THERE have been many who have been kind in encouragement and wise in counsel during the planning and writing of this book. Not only close friends but casual acquaintances have provided spirit for me with their own enthusiasm. To all of those who were glad that I was doing the book, my thanks.

And, more specifically, I am deeply indebted to the *Evening and Sunday Bulletin* and the Philadelphia *Inquirer* for their kind permission to reprint material which appeared originally in their pages. These newspaper pieces of mine, largely from my columns and frequently changed or altered, I have used whenever I felt that they served as significant snapshots for this album, which, I hope, presents the big picture of Philadelphia.

Two books have been invaluable in the work, and again I owe thanks to my newspaper—for the *Bulletin Almanac*, which puts so many vital facts and figures within arm's reach; and *100 Years in Philadelphia:* the *Evening Bulletin's Anniversary Book (1847 to 1947)*, a delightful gallery of pictures with terse, informative captions authored by former staff member Don Fairbairn.

Nobody would—and certainly should not—think of writing about Philadelphia without reading, again, *Philadelphia, Holy Experiment*, by Struthers Burt (Doubleday & Co., Inc., 1945), a rich and rewarding experience; or the chapter on "Philadelphia: Where Patience Is a Vice," by that topflight former newspaperman Thomas P. O'Neil in *Our Fair City*, edited by Colonel Robert S. Allen (Vanguard Press, Inc., 1947).

The *Bulletin* library has been helpful, as always, and I owe a big thank you to its Bernie Landolfi for help and suggestions above and beyond the call of friendship.

Similar big thank yous for help and suggestions are owed to Jerry Katz, Rex Polier, Sid Gathrid, Wayne Robinson, Stuart Taylor, E. Z. Dimitman, Sam Bushman, and Carol Gelber.

My thanks also for help and suggestions to Jack Fleet, Sheldon Rainey, Joe Brooks, Reggie Beauchamp, Milton Bracker, Elizabeth Thompson, Frank Donohoe, Max de Schauensee, Ed Pollock, Ruth Seltzer, Jim Leaming, Herm Fishman, Bill Benson, Joe Gormley, Arnold Stark, Joe Molloy, Pierre Fraley, and Laura Lee.

Another hearty thank you I gratefully offer to my Doubleday editor, Harold Kuebler, without whose infectious enthusiasm the book would never have been started and whose understanding helped so much in carrying it through to completion.

And a special thank you goes to my wife Helen for kindness and understanding above and beyond the call of wifehood throughout the siege at the typewriter.

I can only hope that readers will like the book. If they don't, none of the above-named individuals is to be blamed. Only me.

Contents

Our Philadelphia: A Candid and Colorful Portrait of a Great City

Prologue

"I Spent a Week in Philly One Sunday"

MANY remarks have been made about Philadelphia. Some of them have been true. A lot of the remarks have been nasty. Some of these have been true, too.

Back in 1903 a wonderful reporter named Lincoln Steffens called the city "corrupt and contented." It was. It is not nearly so corrupt now as it used to be. As cities go, in fact, it is much better than most in its municipal government. It is, still, contented.

Another remark you have heard about Philadelphia is:

"I came to Philly on Sunday but it was closed."

Still another is:

"Oh sure, I spent a week in Philly one Sunday."

The most recent gag I have heard along this same cutting line was being passed around at the height of the popularity of the giveaway shows on television. First prize on one of the shows, the gag went, was a week in Philadelphia. The second prize was two weeks in Philadelphia.

But I think the best remarks I have heard about the city came from a southern stranger I met one evening not too long ago in the Celebrity Room, a midtown night club. His name is Lloyd I. Mitchell and he is in the general engineering department of the National Lead Company in New York. He had lived here for business reasons for a period of sixteen months. He had lived in many other places, too.

"Philly," he told me, "is a dead town.

"But," he added quickly, "it's a human town.

"It's better than New York," he said. "It's not so crazy. I've been in New York and I've been in Vegas and I've been in a lot of other places.

"And let me tell you, Philadelphia is real. It's wonderful to be in.

"I'll tell you, it's a lot like the little town I came from in Alabama. It's bigger, but it's a lot like it."

Mr. Mitchell from Alabama hit that old nail squarely on the head. He made the points about the City of Brotherly Love. It *is* real, and it *is* human, and it *is* like a little town. As a matter of fact, for a moment I thought he might have made this book unnecessary. But there *are* some other things to say about the big town in which I live.

Chapter I

So Why Live in the Place?

PHILADELPHIA, home of Hubert B. Wolfeschlegelsteinhausenbergerdorff, Sr.—like Benjamin Franklin a typesetter—and 2,071,604 other residents, according to the last official census in 1950, is the third largest city in the United States of America and the biggest small town in the world.

It was founded in 1682 by a Quaker named William Penn and it is an old city.

It was the cradle of American freedom and it is an historic city.

It covers an area of 129.71 square miles and it is a sprawling city.

It has been called, quite accurately, the City of Homes. But many of its homes are unfit for human habitation.

It is a city of neighborhoods, although some of them have become so rundown in recent years that they somewhat resemble slums.

It has been called the City of Brotherly Love and, to an impressive extent, that is accurate. It is swift to answer any appeal for help, its people are a kindly people—as William Penn and his followers were—but it is slow to change and it is satisfied not to change most of the time.

It is steadily serene, often leisurely and frequently exasperating.

Its climate is awful. It may not get as hot as Washington or St. Louis, but it is miserably humid in the summertime, maliciously damp in the winter months and completely unpredictable any old time of the year.

As early as 1874 its citizens started to desert it in the soggy summer months, heading for Atlantic City and the cool breezes from the ocean; and they have been leaving it in droves every summer week end since that time, hurrying to all of the shore resorts that have grown up in nearby South Jersey points. When the mercury starts soaring into the high temperatures and is accompanied invariably by its oppressive partner, the humidity, Philadelphia takes on the appearance of a ghost town—or city—during the week ends. Almost everybody's gone from its sticky air and heat-shedding streets except the cop on the corner and the derelict in the Tenderloin.

Its transportation system is frequently an inefficient one and something always seems to be breaking down on the Broad Street subway or the Frankford "El." PTC RIDERS DELAYED AT PEAK TRAFFIC HOUR is a familiar headline to the citizens. And certainly the Philadelphia Transportation Co., which operates the transit system, could be called the Banana Line at times, these times being whenever a drop of rain or a bit of snow falls. At these times the trolleys and buses invariably travel in bunches.

When a big snow strikes the city, hardly anything moves, including the horn-honking motorists who just aren't familar with the man-size snows that arrive in other parts of the country. If a bomb ever hit, nothing would move.

The PTC has been constantly plagued by sudden, usually unauthorized walkouts which cripple service temporarily. And the PTC and the city government are always quarreling with each other. The quarrels seem to end like taproom arguments. Nobody wins.

On the other hand, suburbanites get a break in Philadelphia. Where most other cities are complaining about their suburban trains—pity the poor Long Island riders—the Reading Company and the Pennsylvania Railroad furnish good service. The Pennsy's Main Line train, the famous Paoli Local of the commuters' world, is beautifully efficient. One reason for this pleasant state of affiairs, it has been said, is that all the Pennsy executives live out that way. It has been said further that some of the Paoli Local's stops were even created for these esteemed gentlemen.

Philadelphia, like so many other cities, is in the midst of a traffic crisis. High-speed public transportation facilities have not been developed. Private automobiles have clogged the streets. Nothing moves swiftly. There is hope for improvement in a new $976,715 program now under way to change the traffic signal system in the central city. But for years the traffic light system has been so archaic that even Hickville, U.S.A., would have laughed it into the limbo. A motorist might be forced to stop and start five or six times within one small block at a busy hour by lights that were timed to change too quickly. Additionally, the inevitable parking problem and the narrowness of the streets shaded by the skyscraper buildings have made midtown driving a misery.

Nor can pedestrians be absolved of all blame. They are a peculiar breed in the city. And for every horn-honking driver there are at least two pedestrians who are completely disdainful of approaching cars and proceed across the street leisurely in the path of machines making right or left turns, ready to answer a motorist's shout with a pedestrian's sneer. As a cabbie once remarked to me: "They must think these cabs come equipped with rubber bumpers here in Philly."

Philadelphia's municipal government, long a target for well-deserved ridicule, has improved considerably since a reform-minded Democratic party took over control in 1952 after sixty-seven uninterrupted years of shabby Republican rule—or misrule—as the climax to a rebellion by voters simply unable to be "contented" with corruption any longer.

The changes instituted by the progressive and aggressive Democrats, under the youthful leadership of present U.S. Senator Joseph S. Clark, Jr., and current Mayor Richardson Dilworth, haven't been a cure-all, naturally. But more of a premium is placed on honesty and efficiency and service to the taxpayer. Graft, once almost a matter of routine with the ghost of Boies Penrose flitting through the City Hall corridors, has been cut down considerably in many departments. And improvements always are being attempted, at least.

City Hall officeholders, however, have not changed in one respect. They retain one familiar characteristic, it appears. They are, almost invariably, headline hunters. They will make a high-sounding statement at the drop of a question, eyes lighting with the mental image of their names in bold newspaper type.

The Mayor, who incidentally is a fighter and a liberal and a gentleman who will trade hot words with anybody, even took over the hours-long show of a late hour radio spieler for one night when that personality was on vacation.

Philadelphia is always having probes.

PROBE ORDERED is a headline the newspapers—the highly respected *Evening and Sunday Bulletin*, the hard-hitting *Inquirer*, and the now spirited tabloid, the *Daily News*—could keep in type. But rarely does anything concrete or significant come out of the probes, which are usually "sweeping" or "intensive." To some extent there is something of an unwritten law which the city has followed in affairs like these, unless the crime is too reprehensible or the practice too deplorable. The law or policy could be described as Live and Let Live.

The city's big boxing promoter for many years has been an elderly, easygoing, well-liked fellow named Herman (Muggsy) Taylor, who hates his nickname and is proud of the championship fights he has staged. One fight a couple of years ago raised a startling and strange aroma of orange petals. The first-round victim, Harold Johnson, reportedly had been slipped a doped orange, which, unfortunately, he ate just before the bout.

The State Athletic Commission decided to make headline hay by hollering horrors. Taylor, a well-known figure in the city from numerous previous stories, was charged with associating with known racketeers, and the commission sought—unsuccessfully—to revoke his promoter's license.

And who turned up as a character witness for Taylor? Why, none other than His Honor, the Mayor. The same Mayor who had first jumped into the public spotlight as a fearless crusader against the rackets. Some good citizens were a bit dismayed, but nobody was really surprised.

That's the way things happen in Philly sometimes. It can be a city of paradox and contradictions.

At the present time, for instance, it does have a nice class of cops. It has the youngest, best-looking policemen in its history. They are clean-cut, well-spoken and, for the most part, helpful and courteous. But they have the damnedest time solving murders. As a matter of fact, they have solved very, very few of the many, many big ones in the last six years or so. One big reason is that there are so few of the older, not so good-looking, not so well-spoken veterans left in the Police Department.

When former Mayor Clark, the present U.S. Senator, assumed charge of City Hall, he appointed as his Police Commissioner an earnest, honest and well-meaning officer named Thomas P. Gibbons, whose previous experience, however, had been largely with juvenile crime prevention. And when Commissioner Gibbons assumed charge of the department, he immediately introduced drastic changes in procedure and policy, with the result that most of the old-timers retired or quit. Just about the only veteran remaining who has the stool pigeons and the underworld contacts so valuable to any police setup is Captain Clarence R. Ferguson.

Consequently, the situation has been this: A lot of young guys still have a lot to learn—and the unsolved murder list has been a growing one. It reached a ridiculous point in the slaying of a small-time racket operator named Marshall Veneziale, said to have been a still-installer for a bootleg mob.

On December 6, 1954, Veneziale drove away from his South Philly home in his brother's car. The car was found abandoned on a street two miles away early in the morning of December 17. It had been parked there for two days before police, who had the license number, discovered it. And it wasn't until fourteen hours after the discovery of the car that detectives finally thought to look in the trunk. When they did, there, lo and behold, was the body of the missing man, the slain victim they had been looking for. They finally had the corpus delicti but they never did catch up with the hoodlum who had provided it.

In all, thirty policemen were cited by an angry Commissioner Gibbons for neglect of duty. By January the case against a batch of them had been dropped and in March the remaining thirteen were cleared by the police trial board. Not that Philadelphia has the worst cops in the country. It doesn't.

It does have the worst baseball fans.

Although Del Ennis, now of the St. Louis Cardinals, was a local boy from Olney High and the club's leading slugger and RBI man from the time he broke in, he was booed unmercifully. The same treatment was handed out to handy Andy Seminick, a scrappy, hard-working catcher for many years. Subsequently, as if to expiate their guilt and atone for previous sins, the fans staged impressive Nights for both Del and Andy, who had been two of the heroes of the Phillies when they became the Whiz Kids and surprised the nation by winning a National League pennant in 1950. That season the fans were as wild and happy as high school rooters. The Whiz Kids fizzed after that glorious year and the fans have since settled back to normalcy.

It is true that Philadelphia, in the past, spent $25,000,000 on subways that were never operated.

It is true that it built a Municipal Stadium seating 104,000 spectators in a swampland at the southern tip of the city and that about the only event staged there now is the Army-Navy game, a highlight of the year pictorially and a godsend financially.

It is true that, today, the city's planning is not always masterful.

The *Philadelphia Bulletin*—largest evening newspaper in the nation, incidentally—rarely raises its voice in bitter anger. But that newspaper in an editorial early in 1957 described it thusly:

"Philadelphia," it said, "has a tradition in its public works that is being well maintained on the Schuylkill Expressway—a habit of doing things in a disjointed way.

"This is particularly true with the bridges it builds. Virtually a generation was required after the Benjamin Franklin Bridge was built before there were adequate approaches. The Vine Street bridge over the Schuylkill has been completed for some time, but on the west side there's no place to go . . ."

It is true that, today, the city has water and gas main breaks by the scores every year. Its streets are always caving in. Its sewers are always backing up and making big puddles for pedestrians to wade through.

There aren't enough cops on the beat anywhere in the city and holdups, muggings and robberies are at a high peak, many of them taking place on the busiest midtown streets.

Its water, which has been described as "chlorine cocktails" and "Schuylkill Punch," does come from that often malodorous stream cutting right through the city and is enough to drive any person to a wine cellar.

It wouldn't think of putting twenty-four-hour shifts on important public building projects.

It repairs its busiest streets at peak traffic hours.

It can be a hell of an exasperating city.

And all of this perhaps poses a question about Philadelphia. To wit:

Why do people live in it?

Chapter II

Who Would Want to Live Anywhere Else?

You could say that we love the historic old lady despite her faults, and that would be true. She has plenty of faults, granted. We still love her. But we don't boast about her.

Philadelphians don't make a habit of shouting their feelings about their city loudly. If it's possible to ruffle a Texan, they would drive one to distraction. They accept all of the gags about their city, the ridicule, the disparagement, the fun poked at it, with a kind of benign smile. They admit that there may be substance for many of the gags and soundness in some of the ridicule. And they smile again, somewhat as though they know a secret much too big and precious to be shared with any outsider.

What they are saying then, in effect, is: So what? It's nice living here. And it is.

Perhaps it is something like a guy with a girl. She may not be real pretty, say, but she smiles a certain way. Or her nose may be a trifle too large but she has an understanding expression. Anyway, the gal wins the guy and he's happy and he knows he loves her, but he would find it difficult to explain why completely. There is a certain way about her, that is all he knows.

Philadelphia has a way about her, too, and I think primarily it is this: Philadelphia is a small town. A big town but a small town. It appeals to its people because of its old-fashioned charm, its casual slowness and the comparative leisure which remains possible in its busy metropolitan life. Its oldness, its familiarity, even its many unchanging ways, endear it to its residents. But basically, and above all, we like it because of its small-town flavor.

Your Philadelphian is a city dweller who can nonetheless, to a remarkable degree, lead the life of a small towner. The big reasons for this are that it is a city of homes, with little lawns to tend and house repairs to make; and it is a city of distinct and individual neighborhoods, with sectional lodges, organizations, veterans' groups and churches to join and be active in.

True, the topography has changed. The old and ugly "Chinese Wall," which once carried the Pennsy's tracks out to the newer and brighter Thirtieth Street Station from the long dismantled Broad Street Station, was torn down. In the blocks of the midtown opened up by the demolishment of the "Wall" there has risen a magnificent example of urban redevelopment—Penn Center. Included in this Penn Center are new office buildings, the new 22-story, 1,000-room, $16,000,000 Sheraton Hotel, the new Transportation Center and other structures which have given a genuinely New Look to City Hall's immediate environs.

An ironic aspect to the building of the Penn Center is that right across from its glistening, handsome, modern edifices lies the honky-tonk stretch of Market Street, with a conglomeration of gaudy, neon-lighted penny arcades, pinball palaces, cheap shops and hot dog and orange drink stands.

Toward the Delaware River another redevelopment program, the Independence Mall, has brought modern beauty to the area surrounding the old historic shrines.

And, since the end of World War II, large and luxurious apartment houses have sprung up like giant wild plants in the panoramic picture of the midtown, particularly around the Benjamin Franklin Parkway and ritzy Rittenhouse Square. With these apartment houses and the housing projects in a city that faced an acute shortage of dwelling space after the war, there has been a tre-

"Old Original" Bookbinders

mendous migration to the suburbs. The new suburban residents have gone out the Main Line through Wynnewood and Radnor and Cynwyd to Valley Forge and its historic countryside and story of valor. To the north they have moved to the quickly created community of Levittown and on up into Bucks County, the rustic refuge for so many well-known personalities engaged in the lively arts in New York. And they have found a new place to live down through the South Jersey towns and land not too long a ride across the Delaware from Philadelphia plants and offices.

Largely these refugees from the city have been the younger families, thousands of World War II veterans, moving from somebody else's old home to a new, speedily constructed one of their own, where there is more fresh air for their children and more space in which those growing youngsters can play. The migration to the suburbs, the new shopping centers and the department store branches that come with it, is a story in itself, of course, but it is part of a national story, a trend apparent all across Uncle Sam's rich and varied landscape.

But in Philadelphia there has been, with the exodus by thousands of families, the arrival of thousands more, many of them Negroes from the South, seeking a better life and finding it. And Philadelphia has remained a city of homes and of neighborhoods and sections, so many sections . . .

The mill sections of Kensington (Kitty Foyle's home) and Frankford. Charming old Germantown, scene of an important Revolutionary War battle. West Philly, North Philly. South Philly, teeming, heavily populated, home of the old gangs in days gone past, Murder Alley for the notorious Lanzettis and also the birthplace of so many of America's favorite singers. Old Manayunk and hilly Roxborough. Overbrook, Mayfair, Tacony, Olney, Bridesburg, Richmond, Wissinoming, the Northeast, Wynnefield, Rhawnhurst, Holmesburg, Torresdale, Lawndale, Eastwick, Southwest Philly, Oak Lane, Mt. Airy. Social Chestnut Hill. Logan, named for James Logan, who came to the town in 1699 at the age of twenty-five as secretary to William Penn and became a powerful figure. East Falls, former home of a princess, Princess Grace of Monaco, John B. Kelly's pretty daughter and one member of the big town's most famous family. And Strawberry Mansion and Nicetown and Fishtown and Brewerytown . . .

Each of these is a small town in itself. When I moved from an apartment in Overbrook, where I had lived for some twelve years —ever since my marriage—I felt almost like Sherwood Anderson's young man leaving "Winesburg, Ohio." I felt as though I were leaving a town, when in fact I was only moving some forty or so city blocks.

"This one," I wrote for the column that day, "is not from our regular corner in the city room but from a new place to live in —on Moving Day—and it is put down with a certain amount of sadness.

"Neighborhoods in our big city are like small towns in our country and, after twelve years, it is not easy to leave a neighborhood.

"This, then, is sort of a quiet farewell to the people in the 'town,' the people we have been seeing and saying hello to and knowing and talking to and laughing with for a long time now, because we won't be seeing them so much in the future.

"The place that was our home from 1939 until yesterday wasn't too much, nothing fancy, just a nice little apartment. But, on two occasions, we recall, it seemed very much like a palace.

"The first time was on the dreary dawn in which we went off to join an Army Uncle Sam was getting together. The second time was nearly three years later, on the bright and wonderful evening when we came back from the ETO and resumed once more that most magnificent role in the world—that of being a free man.

"Thomas Wolfe had woven a spell about trains and that was one reason we moved into the old place. That was the poetic reason. There is always the practical one, too—the rent.

"The roar of the express trains zooming through the night and the shuttling of the freights on the tracks off Lancaster Avenue have brought their rewards—the novelist did not steer us wrong— and they have also brought with them a considerable amount of smoke. Final score: The two balanced each other.

"Through the years we have had innumerable discussions with Yank Quinn about this smoke business. Yank is a short little guy, who reads a great deal and is a veteran PRR engineer. He always said he was giving out orders not to have any smoke tossed at our place. He even said that he might take it up with Martin W. Clement, Esq.

"The smoke remained with us to the end, however. But you could never see it in the nights—and you could hear those trains hurtling through the darkness for faraway places.

"Mr. Hoffman is the tailor down the street. He has been ill lately, and we wish him the best. The day before we went into the Army, he stopped over and told the girl who was staying behind: 'If you have trouble, if the money gets short, just let the bills go until he comes back.'

"Mr. Gottlieb, who runs the delicatessen across the street, is a man of wry humor. One afternoon he was digging deep into the frozen foods box for something. He had just about every package out and was still digging for the one he wanted. 'What are you looking for?' asked his wife. 'A million dollars,' said Mr. Gottlieb —and kept on looking.

". . . One Sunday afternoon, a good day indeed, the girl in our place came home with a bountiful smile and a tiny bundle in her arms. 'Look,' she said very tenderly, 'here he is.'

"The bundle was fat and bouncy—and it had sad eyes that changed quickly to eyes full of mischief, and it turned out to be a puppy named Muggs, who has grown up to be a very fine dog, just as full of love as he is of the devil.

"As with the trains, the score is even, balanced, although we have lost from our wardrobe two pairs of shoes, one pair of slippers, and sundry other items. The many gains would include hundreds of good laughs.

"Once it was trains and now, you might say, it is Muggs.

"The new place isn't too much, nothing fancy, just a nice little apartment.

"But it is bigger than the old one and it is first floor and it has a little backyard for Muggs. He rates it.

"Lou Wool says he'll bring Rex down so they can renew old friendships. Tony Turtzo, we'll be up next week for our haircut.

"Meanwhile, there will be a lot of new people to meet, new butcher, new baker, new candlestick maker.

"And the new place is fine. It's home.

"And we hope you will pardon us for not having been impersonal in the customary way this morning. We wanted to say a little good-by to an old neighborhood. Next time out we'll be back to normalcy, trying to tell about a lot of things in a lot of 'small towns' in our big city."

And, the more important point I made earlier, each of these small towns adds up to one big small town. For, more than any other city in the country, I think, Philadelphia (with a metropolitan population of 3,671,048) has the spirit of a small town, the friendliness, the neighborliness, the hospitality, the generosity—even the corner talk, the desire to stop for a little conversation, a little get-together.

The meetings of the Kiwanis, the Rotary, the Ladies' Aid Society in a small town are duplicated by the hundreds each noontime and night in Philadelphia by its scores of American Legion and Veterans of Foreign War posts, its business organizations, its booster clubs, its Knights of Columbus councils, its B'nai B'rith and B'rith Shalom lodges, its little theater groups in every section, its Home and School Associations, its testimonial dinners for a public figure or a retiring employee, its hundreds of social, political, charitable, welfare, intellectual and simply neighborly groups.

Philadelphia loves its luncheon affairs and its evening banquets, its annual dinners and its Christmas parties. Its people love to get together.

There is the quiet of a small town, too, in this city. Not in the daytime, naturally, for the city is the fourth largest manufacturing workshop in the country (87 per cent of all industrial classifications may be found here), its port is the second biggest in the nation, and it is a busy banking, business, shipbuilding and shopping center. But, except on Wednesday shopping nights, the hurried footsteps of the multitudes which have trod the skyscraper canyons during the rushing daytime hours fade into the casual walk of the few, come evening.

Philadelphians do not rush back into their midtown after they have finished the day's work there—except, largely, those who are going to a play or a movie. They do not turn it into a Forty-second and Broadway. For the most part they stay at home or gather in the neighborhood taproom.

Many nights the midtown streets of the city are as quiet as Main Street. There is a brief flurry of heavy traffic, a quick rush of business for the cabbies, after the theaters have broken, after the music has ended at the old Academy of Music. But by midnight there is nothing much but silence. Philadelphians are not stay-up-lates.

There is the quiet of a small-town Sunday in our city, too. That may be old-fashioned in our tense and bustling day and age, but it also has an appealing charm. Because of the state liquor laws, all of the bars are closed. Consequently, there is less noise in the hotels, less loud chatter in the restaurants and less turmoil on the streets. Sunday becomes a day for family visiting, for attending sports events, for cutting the grass, for washing and shining the car in front of the house and for going to church. A lazy stillness lies over the streets. It really seems like Sunday in Philadelphia.

Fairmount Park helps, too, to give the city a small-town atmosphere, although this lovely vista of wooded slopes and rolling hills and Wissahickon Creek and the ever-present Schuylkill and motorists' drives along that river and bridle paths and trails and bridges and small lakes and genuine country scenes, is larger in itself than many cities. It covers more than 4,000 acres, is the largest municipally owned park (within a city proper) in the country, and yet sends its welcome messages from nature right into the heart of the city, being connected casually to the business section by the one-mile stretch of the Parkway that is the road to work and the quick way home for thousands of midtown workers. And here can be found the family picnics and the Sunday picnics in the summertime and the beauty of the hills beyond a town when fall arrives.

But mostly Philadelphia is a small town because of its people. They have many of the ways, much of the outlook, many of the attitudes and much of the warmth and friendliness of the people who live in the small towns of America.

Chapter III

Meet Some People in Our Town

LET me try to explain about Philadelphia.

There is a veterinarian in our town named Dr. Leonard Krawitz. A young man, he operates the West Park Animal Hospital on Lansdowne Avenue, teaches at the University of Pennsylvania and is one of the finest veterinarians in our country. He is devoted to animals and dedicated to his work with them. As his wife says, she has never had a real vacation because he always chooses a time when a convention is being held so that he can attend it and learn more about taking care of animals. She goes along. It isn't the usual vacation a wife expects but she would not have it any other way, being Mrs. Krawitz.

Back around Thanksgiving time in 1955 my wife and I bundled our dog Muggsy into a big blanket and were driven to Dr. Krawitz' hospital by our friend from next door, Arnold Stark. We knew that Muggsy was very sick. Another veterinarian unfortunately had diagnosed his ailment incorrectly. We did not know that Muggsy was dying.

Dr. Krawitz quickly diagnosed the little fellow's trouble as nephritis. He went to work swiftly, efficiently. Drugs were needed.

Drugs were gotten. Everything possible was done. The staff went to work with Dr. Krawitz, whom I had never met until that day We did not learn about it until later but two of them stayed up all night with Muggsy that first night he was in the hospital, voluntarily, dividing shifts, so that somebody would be ready if something went wrong.

Dr. Krawitz saved Muggsy's life. That is the important part of the story but it is not the reason why I am telling about Dr. Krawitz. That Christmas my wife and I, hearts happy with Muggsy around and filled with gratitude that he was, sent a large basket of fruit to the doctor and his staff.

The card with it said: "Many thanks and merry Christmas—Muggsy."

Muggsy received a note of thanks.

Again at Christmas time in 1956 we sent a basket of fruit from Muggs. As before, the letter from a very busy veterinarian was addressed to "Mr. Muggs B——." It read:

Dear Muggs—

Your surprise gift basket of fruit, which was delivered in prime condition Christmas Eve, brought delight to all of us. Please know that your wonderful gesture was deeply appreciated.

I know that you are only on a small weekly allowance, and I know that this gift could only have been made possible through the efforts of really wonderful people who obviously hold you in high regard.

You can do me a great favor by thanking them *personally*—for me and my family.

We all join in wishing you a Healthy and Happy 1957.

Sincerely—Doc.

So you will never be able to tell me that the old family doctor or the old country doctor has gone out of style. Not so long as Dr. Krawitz continues to save the lives of dogs and cats and canaries and even raccoons on Lansdowne Avenue in Philadelphia.

When a handsome, black-haired young man named Jimmy Ercolani was a high school boy, he loafed around Sam's Luncheonette at Tenth and Wolf Streets in the section of South Philly which has provided the nation with so many of its entertainers. Jimmy Ercolani, of South Philly, became James Darren, of Hollywood.

When movie star James Darren made personal appearances at the Stanton Theater in the midtown for the opening of his first picture, a quickly forgotten opus called *Rumble on the Docks,* Sam Mangarola closed down his luncheonette that night for the first time in honor of the opening. He took a party of forty to the theater. The members of the party, all old friends of Jimmy Ercolani, whistled and applauded almost every time he spoke a line. Some of them said that this James Darren movie was the best one they had ever seen, which just goes to show how wrong critics can be at times.

One of the most frequent and steady contributors to the Letters to the Editor columns of the Philadelphia newspapers is Mayor Dilworth. A spirited and aggressive gentleman who is both loudly lauded and bitterly blasted by the citizenry, Dilworth first rode into public office by ripping into the GOP regime (which deserved it), the racket setup (which made good headlines) and his opponents (who were often proper targets) in dramatic and exciting street corner talks.

He has quieted down some since he became Mayor and the worth-while letters are written to defend a step taken or explain an action planned. A typical example would go like this:

"I read with interest the editorial in last Sunday's *Bulletin* . . . Actually, the Delaware Expressway poses no real threat to the historic homes of Elfreth's Alley, and I can assure those . . . The situation as it now stands is this . . ."

His Honor, of course, is accused by some of thus campaigning all the year round. But it strikes me that it's a healthy business—something like the Burgess (they are Burgesses in Pennsylvania) of a small town explaining some action of his to a group of factory laborers or coal miners on a Main Street corner.

Some six years ago I dutifully reported in the column that a new sign had appeared in the window of the office of optician Robert S. Valent at 1809 Snyder Avenue.

The sign said: "Closed for day—wife has TWINS."

Three years later the column again reported that another new sign had appeared in the same office window. This one said: Closed for half a day—wife has only one baby this time."

Robert S. Valent is still keeping the people posted. In 1956 the column was once more happy to report the appearance of another sign in the same window. This one carried a longer message. It said:

"Closed for an extra hour at lunch time to see wife and new baby. Can't afford to close for any longer with FOUR children to maintain."

One morning a society note arrived at my desk. It read:

"Mr. A. Virgilio Inzillo of 912 Day st., Phila., Pa., took a trip to Italy on June 16, 1950 to see people that he has not seen for Forty-Six yrs. He is coming back home Sept. 18, 1950, on the SS Saturnia arriving in New York.

"Mr. A. Virgilio Inzillo has raised six children. He has been working as a Stone Mason since he was sixteen yrs. old. One of his sons Dominic T. Inzillo will go to New York on Sept. 18, 1950 to meet his father."

The item was printed that way. It was brief, to be sure. But all of the essential facts were there. Tersely and quietly, it managed to picture the life and work and career of A. Virgilio Inzillo. It also told of the little dream that he had had for many years—to see his native land again. The life, the work, the career, the dream —all of them in a couple of quiet paragraphs. There was nothing, really, for me to add except—A good journey home, Mr. Inzillo!

Sometimes I feel like a small-town editor.

Many nights in Philadelphia are like a small-town night. You get to know the boys and girls by face as you walk in the neighborhood. One recent evening as I was taking Muggsy for a stroll we met two of our little friends. Singularly blessed are the young at heart, I thought that evening. They need only a pocketful of dreams and imagination to become swashbuckling, unconquerable heroes moving about the world—on a drab city street.

These two boys were playing on a stairway leading from a first-floor apartment in an old corner house to the cement street, and both of them at the moment were swinging on the iron rail at the top of it. They are always having some adventure, these two little friends of ours. They are cowboys and Indians. They are firing a machine gun in a war. They are attacking cattle rustlers. They are launching a space ship. They are hitting a home run to win a game at Yankee Stadium. They are taking off for the moon—and they are all the heroes of the world rolled into two little boys.

"What are you playing tonight?" I asked.

"Navy," said Freckle Face, with a giant-size grin.

"The Navy's on the sea," said this old man with nothing in his pockets but change and keys. "You can't play it on the land."

"Sure we can," said Freckle Face. "I'm the captain of a Marine outfit and he [his pal] is the skipper of the LST taking us into the island."

And they went on swinging on the rail of this LST on the drab city street, headed for war with no fear in their hearts. Ocean waves rolled all around us on the cement sidewalk and daring and bravery were rampant in the neighborhood as I walked on with Muggsy.

He, too, plays at games, and is young at heart. He will stalk and attack and bark at an ordinary little biscuit on the living-room floor, turning it into a fierce and giant cat, a veritable tiger, before he conquers and consumes it, tail wagging merrily all the time. And watching first the boys and then Muggsy, I felt a little younger. No hero. But a little younger.

It was a good night.

One hot summer afternoon some years ago I happened to pass the Railway Express Co. loading platform at Thirtieth and Walnut streets. A gang of rugged-looking men were shoving heavy crates aboard the waiting trucks—and they were hotter than the weather. Their faces were grim and unsmiling. Their shirts were soaked with perspiration. Their voices were loud. And their words wouldn't have made a hit at a church social.

Then suddenly everything changed.

The big, rough guys came to one crate and all at once the hot afternoon wore a completely different complexion. Work stopped for a little while. The guys hovered over the crate and they began to smile. Their voices became soft, and some of them spoke words that were plain old baby talk. They weren't thinking of the heat now. They weren't bothered by their work any more. Because, commanding their attention and concern in the crate, was a sad-faced little puppy dog, bound for some distant spot, looking lonely and confused about the journey ahead.

So the big, rough sweaty guys spoke their words of affection and assurance. "Everything's going to be all right, little feller," one said softly and with tenderness to give the puppy courage for its journey. And discovering suddenly that it had a lot of big, solid friends in the world, the little dog wagged its tail.

It was a good afternoon.

There was no doubt about it. Old Buck was a ham. He missed the spotlight. He yearned for a chance to perform again for those big audiences. He wanted to strut his stuff once more in front of thousands of televiewers. But the show was ended, his career was finished—and it hurt an actor like Old Buck.

See, Old Buck had never really been a member of the horsy set. They had never displayed all of his fine points at the fancy shows. He was just a fifteen-year-old buckskin-colored cow pony out at Jack Segal's Fair-Mount Stables. And all of his life he had never been much except just another horse. Then WCAU-TV started a network show called "Action in the Afternoon," a real live Western, and that shoved Old Buck into the world of glamour and grease paint for the first time. All of the horses for the television show were rented from the Fair-Mount Stables, and Old Buck galloped out of obscurity.

For a year he cavorted for the thousands, and it got into his blood, and it stayed. The show went off the television screens finally, but Old Buck continued to report for his acting chores. After that last show he ran away from the stables two or three times a week, strolled the mile from the stables to the television station, crossed heavily traveled City Line and wound up at the spot where the outdoor set for "Action in the Afternoon" had been located.

It was never any trouble to locate him. The Fair-Mount Stables would just send somebody over to WCAU-TV in a car to take him back. "Old Buck's gone again," they would say. And they knew that he would be over there at the set, wanting to make some "Action in the Afternoon," waiting for—lights, camera, action! Sure, he was a ham at heart. But what's wrong with an unsung, unglamorous, undistinguished old cow pony dreaming of some real Kentucky Derby-style glory?

Here I started out to tell about Philadelphians and I was sidetracked by a puppy dog and an old cow pony. But there are some other people I want you to know, because they are the way Philadelphia is.

There is, for one, a big, easygoing, goodhearted gentleman named Mort Farr. He is a big electrical appliance dealer on Sixty-ninth Street, the oldest of the suburban shopping sections. He is a past president and present board chairman of the National Association of Retail and Appliance Dealers. He is also the sponsor of my Sunday night television show. The show, for which Mort does his own commercials, has been on the air for more than six years now.

We have never had a contract. "We'll shake hands on it," Mort said when the show began. And that's all there has ever been—a handshake.

To my desk early in 1957 came this letter from Herman Lebowitz, a newsboy at Eleventh and Market streets:

I would like to give a thanks to the firemen who put out the fire at my Newstand on the South East Corner of 11th & Market Street, on February 14, 1957.

Also I would like to thank Edward Bergen of the Police Department. He notified me at my home about the fire at my newstand.

Sincerely yours—Herman Lebowitz.

A Philadelphia song writer named Frankie Capano, whose biggest hit was one called "Tears" from many years back, was a good friend of mine. Not a close friend, but a good friend. He always liked to buy me a tie when he went to New York on a business trip. I pleaded with him not to do it. Each time he did it. He said he enjoyed doing it. And he continued to do it even when he was having hard times. He continued to do it right up until the time when he could no longer go to New York because of his diabetes and a heart condition that finally took his life—without having taken away his good spirit—in the summer of 1956.

I had never met his son and do not know him now. But that Christmas I received a tie from Frank Capano, Jr.

Sometimes I feel like a small-town editor.

Chapter IV

It's Much Bigger Than a Village

As MUCH as Philadelphia has the neighborliness of a small town, it is, of course, not a small town but a big city. And a lot of people get lost in it. So it is inevitable that an old small-town boy who has always been fascinated by and interested in people, in knowing about their lives and why they are the way they are, cannot be reconciled completely to life in the big city. There is too much he doesn't know or cannot learn. Too many people hurry down the street, too many people appear on a corner and then are gone suddenly. Too many people are never anything but shadows.

A man can die in the big city, only half a block from where you live, and you may not even be aware of it. It gives you a strange, eerie feeling.

This man lived a quiet life, for he was an invalid in a wheel chair, but death came noisily—with fire engines clanging down the street and sirens blasting the peaceful atmosphere of a holiday afternoon. You stepped out on to your porch. You saw the engines come to a stop down the street. But there were no flames, no smoke. It appeared to be a very small fire and, besides, it was a bitter winter day, and so you came in from the porch and closed the door against the cold and returned to the comfort of your living room.

That night you took your dog for a walk and you had forgotten about the fire altogether until you passed the house and saw on the front lawn the pieces of charred furniture that had been a man's home. It must have been a sofa fire, you thought. Doesn't look as though there was much damage.

It was not until the next morning that you came to work and read in your newspaper that a man, "an invalid, died yesterday in a fire that swept the living room of a second floor apartment. . . ."

When you took your dog for a walk later that night, the charred furniture was still there on the lawn, the windows had been boarded up, and a man's life, you knew, was gone. It did not seem right that all you knew about this man, a neighbor, was that he was an invalid and that he had died the day before without your ever having known him, although he lived only half a block away. And you walked past the charred furniture now with a strange, eerie feeling, remembering that you had come in from the porch quickly after the fire engines clanged to a halt. You had closed your door against the cold—a man was dying down the street.

I would like to know a little more about the meek and frail-looking man of about fifty years who used to walk into the Horn & Hardart restaurant at Fifty-fourth and City Line. This place is often jokingly referred to as the Country Club because so many of the women from the suburbs (it is right on the edge of the city) and big homes in Wynnefield wear minks and such when they drop in for coffee after a social affair.

The man, most of the time, was timid and he would simply occupy a counter stool, order his pie and tea, eat and leave. But about once a month he would come into the place considerably under the influence and he would walk from table to table, sneering at the customers.

"Rich fools," he would sneer in a whisper.

And then, having made his point, he would leave.

There was another middle-aged gentleman I saw one day. He was neatly dressed and he carried a briefcase. Looking at him, you would think: He is probably one of those teachers who carries on a life-long courtship with learning, or perhaps one of those minor executives, never slated for advancement, who must present a smart appearance on a shabby salary. His thoughts seemingly on some mountaintop, he walked past the various foods displayed on the counter of the midtown H & H with little or no interest, until he reached the coffee dispenser.

"Just a cup of hot water, please," he told the attendant there, and went on his way with the free liquid.

Seated comfortably then at a table, he opened his briefcase, withdrew a small jar of soluble coffee, and proceeded to brew his own beverage. The coffee ready, he reached further into the briefcase and came out this time with a neatly wrapped sandwich and a copy of an erudite journal. And then he unwrapped his sandwich, opened his magazine, stirred his coffee, and settled down with his lunch and his literature.

Looking at him, you thought: He may be the type of guy who later, when he gets back to the office, will mark in his little notebook: "Lunch—$1.25." But you weren't sure. And you weren't sure about the lunch either. Had it been a planned pleasure, sufficiently rewarding, or a necessary sacrifice? You had a question you couldn't ask a proud old gentleman. And he left with the answer in his briefcase.

Certainly, in a small town, I would know more about this gentleman, who may still be up to his old tricks. He is so wealthy that he could paper his living room with bills if he were in the mood for such a recreational pursuit. His taste, however, runs to another sport, which boasts the added lure of competition—the sharp foray, the swift concealment, the easy prize, triumph or disaster. He is, in short, despite his wealth, a kleptomaniac.

Regularly and always jauntily, he used to saunter into the Evans drugstore at Broad and Locust. There he would have a whirl at his favorite pastime.

He always ordered a cup of coffee and the employees were always ready. They also played the game. They watched his every movement and simply added the cost of articles taken to the coffee check. Sometimes it was only a piece of cake or a candy bar. At other times the gentleman sought a trophy worthy of his skill. He was exceedingly clever and invariably suave.

One day he wrapped two pieces of pound cake in his newspaper. One dropped out. Quickly he turned to the man next to him at the counter.

"Pardon me, sir," he said, "did you drop this cake?"

He always examined his checks for coffee like a sport and he would smile if he found that his coffee had cost him perhaps 57 cents, or 68 cents, or $1.35.

"Oh very well," he would say, admitting defeat. The victories—if there were any—he treasured to himself. In *le sport* one must always be the gracious loser, the modest winner. And the gentleman is a gentleman.

These people, and many others, remain shadows in a big town.

But it was different with Mr. Ingram. It could easily have been that way with him, too. But he moved out of the shadows in the last days of his life.

Mr. Ingram, a third-floor roomer in the house where we live, died one Friday night about eight years ago and when a cold rain came at the end of Saturday afternoon, it seemed to wash away his life completely. He was a small, friendly, neat and nicely dressed old man who had been alone in the world since the death of his wife, a former actress, some three years before; and he left nobody who was close to him.

We did not know him at all, really, and only talked to him once, on the night, we suppose, when he knew—or felt—for the first time that he was going to die. At first to us, because we were new in the house, he was just the old man upstairs. But every time that he went in or out, he would pass the door to our first-floor apartment and he would always tap on the glass panes to say hello to Muggs. Muggsy, in return, would respond with his own tail-wagging greeting.

And they got to know each other well. Muggsy knew the footsteps and never missed Mr. Ingram when he went out for a lonely meal or came back to his small room to entertain, as he did so many nights, his only companion—his past.

So, in a brief time, he became not the old man upstairs but Mr. Ingram of the third floor. And when he had the stroke and went to the hospital, we missed him and wondered how he was coming along and hoped he would be all right. He had become a part of our daily lives, small but definite.

He did come back from the hospital that time. But only a few days later, in the evening, he came up the porch steps and gestured for help through the window. He asked if he could stay with us—Helen and Muggsy and me—for a while.

"I didn't think I was going to make it," he said. "I don't think I could get up those stairs."

He stayed for an hour before he regained his strength. He watched Muggsy and smiled and said: "We always had a dog in the family when I was a kid." He told us he didn't know what he would have done without Rosalie, the cleaning girl for the second- and third-floor rooms, in the last few weeks. He told us that he had once been a salesman. That, in fact, was the great irony in Mr. Ingram's life. He had been a top traveling salesman and then a year before, when he had suffered his first stroke, his speech had been affected. And where does that leave a salesman?

Mr. Ingram retired to his little room on the third floor. But his appearance was always dapper. People on the street always said how immaculate he seemed. They would have been surprised to learn that there were only two suits in Mr. Ingram's room, neatly hung. And, to be sure, a shoe tree.

That evening when he came into our place he seemed to enjoy being with us—in a living room with television and soft chairs and Muggsy lying there. He said he was sorry he had bothered us and that he was grateful. And we helped him to his room, finally, and that was the last time we saw Mr. Ingram. He went to the hospital again a few days later.

But I have thought many times since then how much one small, friendly gesture—or a kind word or a simple act of kindness—can mean, what a big difference it can make after the death and the cold rains that follow. To us, Mr. Ingram could easily have been

Mr. Nobody, a man without identity. We knew him hardly at all, saw him only for a couple of months, just more or less passing by. But because he always tapped on the door to say hello to Muggsy, a little thing accounting for seconds of time in a life of years, he became a distinct personality.

He will never be Mr. Nobody, never just the old man upstairs. To us, he will always be Mr. Ingram, the nice old man on the third floor. And that way he stays around in our lives.

Chapter V

Taking an Impressionistic Look

PHILADELPHIA is a big city with a vast variety of sights and sounds and smells which are a reflection of its life, its happiness, its richness and its strength. It is many things, It is crowded subways and jammed trolleys at the rush hours beginning and ending the workdays . . . And lazy Sundays.

It is men with lunch pails walking swiftly through the streets . . . Bustling women with their shopping bags on Wednesday nights . . . Growing girls walking home from high schools in bright sweaters and with bouncing conversations . . . Couples strolling on the campuses, books under their arms, great hopes behind their smiles . . . Pop walking proudly with his toddling son in Fairmount Park. And why not proudly? The boy could be President.

It is talkative barbers . . . Bartenders with tin ears from hearing troubles . . . Cabdrivers with ideas. It is big business in a skyscraper and a poet writing beautiful words for peanuts in a basement room. It is the low rumble of a train tearing through the town . . . The shrill siren of fire engines stabbing the night's silence . . . The rattle of milkmen's bottles in the dawn . . .

The tired shouts of small children heading home at dusk . . . A big and hopeless dream suddenly remembered over a small and smoky bar.

It is the strong, enveloping aroma of fresh popcorn from a bright cubbyhole stand on a honky-tonk street . . . Emcees in night clubs singing "Happy Birthday" to somebody nobody knows . . . Faces glued to the television screens in taprooms for a fight . . . The tiny light of a passenger plane riding high in the sky's darkness.

It is boys ready to brave any danger because they have seen Gene Autry and Roy Rogers in action . . . Crunchies for breakfast—and health . . . All of the ad slogans, the ceaseless commercials, the chattering jingles . . . Little boys in Phillies' outfits, the tip of their hats as long as their feet, to whom sluggers with a chaw of tobacco in their mouth and a home run in their bat are idols . . . A fast halfback darting into the open at Franklin Field or the Connie Mack Stadium, bringing the crowd to its collective feet . . . A swisher through the cords from way out at the Palestra . . . The sudden applause for a rally by the home team gaining sweep and power through the stands.

It is the feeling of being close to history and great events, standing outside Independence Hall on a sunny summer afternoon. It is wisecracking waitresses . . . well-groomed hostesses . . . immaculate headwaiters. It is the neighborhood Romeos standing outside the theaters appraising the passing girls, the girls feigning unawareness of the inventory . . . A picnic in Fairmount Park on a hot summer day . . . A boy and girl holding hands with love in a movie . . . All of the new drive-ins around the town . . . The Met at the Academy . . . Store windows jammed with "Specials!" . . . Gas stations, billboards, launderettes, dancing schools.

It is a week-end jaunt to the shore . . . A stop at the confectionery . . . The lusty shout of the corner newsboy with a new edition . . . The slow, deliberate pronouncement of the family doctor . . . The purple prose of the holiday orator . . . The meaningless verbal patter of a tap dancer . . . The soothing introduction to pain by the dentist . . . The busy ladies of the civic clubs . . . The bar belles of the night clubs . . . The lure of the many magazines on the newsstands . . . The parade over the Parkway . . . A kid with a mongrel dog . . . Gossip columns and after-dinner speakers and monthly luncheons. And it is the foam on the beer after a regular hard day's work and the bubbles on champagne for a very special occasion.

There are some other less general things I want to mention, too.

It is a big and varied town, our Philadelphia, and when I think of it, letting the mind rove and the eyes wander, I think of a million things. It is a kaleidoscopic view that results, but all of the parts, of many shapes and sizes and styles, perhaps add up to the big picture.

And it occurs to me when I am assembling these parts, as I am now, that:

Philadelphians are a cold-blooded lot. Not in the mean sense. They are the reverse of that. But they will sit in a trolley car or a bus on the hottest day of the summer and not bother to push up a window for a little air.

Mostly only visitors know that Broad Street, running from north to south, smack into the sprawling Navy Yard, and cutting right through City Hall, is the longest straight street in the world. It's twelve miles long. The residents are probably too busy driving on the street to think of statistics about it.

It rains more often in this town on Wednesdays, when the stores are open late for shopping, than on any other day of the week.

No city in the world has prettier girls than those you see pour out of the offices to parade on Chestnut Street during the business hours of the day.

The shrewdness of our local lawyers has often been commented upon, but it's time that somebody pointed out how long they remain active and stay alert. Prize example: George Wharton Pepper, now ninety years old. And for criminal cases, nobody would turn down a Billy Gray, a nationally known court figure for decades; or a Tom McBride, who is now Pennsylvania's Attorney General. Both are famous in legal circles for winning tough cases with clever maneuvering.

Kids from our slums cavort on a rich playground in one stretch of Fairmount Park—right in front of 2601 Parkway, one of the swank modern apartment houses.

Temple University is considered to be an urban university with sidewalks for a campus. But it has 98.66 acres of grass to cut every summer.

The rumbling old elevated has disappeared west of City Hall as far as Forty-sixth Street and when the steel girders and tracks were torn down in 1956, Market Street took on a new appearance and became a driving delight. But I miss the old trains. The elevated cars moving over the Schuylkill always looked to me like a roller coaster full of merry people. Actually the people were usually gloomy because they were going to work or glum because it had been a hard day in the office or the mill.

Coal trucks unloading at homes on our streets think nothing of holding up trolleys for five minutes or so by blocking the tracks.

Judge Joseph Sloane has always struck me as being the kind of gentleman you expect a good judge to be. He is one of our truly fine citizens.

And they don't come any better than Judge Curtis Bok, who is also an author of note. If he hadn't become a jurist, he would certainly be one of the nation's leading scholars—arts and humanities. As it is, he brings a noble note of intellect, intelligence and common sense to the courtroom.

There is no other city from which you can reach the country so quickly. You don't even have to race to the suburbs. You'll find it in Fairmount Park and Chestnut Hill.

Every city has a wide range of names, but Philadelphia's would be difficult to beat. You can go from Francis Daniel Pastorius, who founded Germantown, to Benny the Bum, the late restaurateur who never believed in menus and was one of Heywood Broun's favorite characters. You can go from those pretty Welsh names (the Welsh were the first Main Liners in town when they settled beyond the Schuylkill in colonial days) like Cynwyd and Gwynedd, right down to Hog Island.

Fishtown belies its name. No section burns with more community pride.

It's a shame that today's youngsters will never have the thrill of riding in one of those open-air summer trolleys to Willow Grove Park.

In our town bus passengers who almost forget their stops and make the driver halt at the last minute get a sneaky smug look on their faces—almost as though they had accomplished something.

Philadelphia ice cream *is* the best and most Philadelphians will tell you it's best *at* the Reading Terminal Market.

There has never been a more tragic sports figure than the late Bill Tilden, who played some of his greatest tennis in the Davis Cup matches staged at the Germantown Cricket Club.

Nobody ever hit a baseball harder than the late Jim Tabor, the Phillies' postwar third baseman.

San Francisco should climb some of our Roxborough streets and then hush up.

There is often more than a shred of truth to a gag. One of the most powerful citizens of our town is financier Albert M. Greenfield, who owns or controls a raft of department stores, hotels, real estate and sundry other properties. Last year this gag was making the rounds: "You hear about it? Greenfield's going to sell the city!"

Trucks can park for hours on our midtown streets to load and unload cargoes, but a cabbie who takes a couple of minutes to load or unload passengers gets a bawling out or a dirty look from the policemen.

In our town when women are shopping in a crowded department store they aren't ladies.

Frank Elster and Benny Sorkin, who are in command of the newsstand on the northwest corner of Thirteenth and Market streets (where you can buy *any* out-of-town or foreign language newspaper), and Johnny Murray, whose stand is on the northeast corner of Broad and Locust streets, are almost as well known to Philadelphians as the proprietor of a newsstand store in a small town.

The greatest spontaneous gag I ever heard was pulled by my warmhearted, good-humored and understanding friend Herman (NMI) Fishman, with whom I went through the war. The first

"Lemon Hill" in Fairmont Park

time our outfit was bombed by the Germans, Herm shook his head and said: "Hey, a guy can get *hurt* in this war!"

Nobody works harder at a hobby than Furey Ellis (and there is a wonderful first name for you), the insurance man who has served eleven consecutive terms as president of the board of trustees of the Philadelphia State Hospital (Byberry) and has built that mental institution from a shambles to an impressive operation.

The sound that symbolizes suburbia today is that of the power lawn mower on a Sunday morning.

Robin Roberts, the Phillies' great right-hander, is a perfect model for any boy in his personal life. And in his own quiet way he is also the best competitor baseball has had since Ty Cobb.

The greatest baseball thrills I ever had came when Dick Sisler hit that home run in the tenth inning in Brooklyn to beat the Bums, 4 to 1, and win a pennant for the Whiz Kids on the last day of the 1950 season; and on that balmy summer night when the Phillies clouted five home runs in one inning, two of them by Andy Seminick, against Cincinnati.

The figure I will remember longest is that of relief ace Jim Konstanty walking in from the bull pen.

Most people think of Philly as a quiet, almost colonial city. But it is also a massive metropolis with plenty of crime on the streets, suicides, stabbings and muggings.

One of the most charming things about the city is that you can walk off a bustling, crowded skyscraper street into a little, old and narrow street—and move from present to past in one step.

No city in the country has three better regular newscasters than John Facenda (WCAU-TV), with his voice as smooth as satin; Taylor Grant (WRCV-TV), an old network hand who came back to the home town; and Gunnar Back (WFIL-TV), a long-time network star who also decided to settle down here.

Nor does any city boast a quicker, wittier or funnier ad-libber than Bob Menefee (WIP) or a Weather Girl prettier than Judy Lee (WRCV-TV).

Nor can any city be ahead of ours in combined contributions to science, culture, industry, education, medicine—and basketball. Let us consider the latter for a moment: The Athletics have moved to Kansas City, the Phillies have faltered since 1950, the professional football Eagles have been having bad years. But the Warriors remain a title contender in professional basketball and, more importantly, Temple, St. Joseph's, Villanova, LaSalle and Penn give the fans the finest collegiate basketball any city could offer. Just from local players of recent years, how would you like to have this team? Tom Gola, Paul Arizin, Hal Lear, Wilt (The Stilt) Chamberlain, Guy Rodgers, Larry Hennessey, Ernie Beck. All Philly products, coach.

It also occurs to me that:

Many people in our town do not know about, or have never been to, some of its most picturesque sections. They have never been to Dock Street, with its litter and its noise, in the early morning hours. They have never been to Manayunk which, despite its homely name, has been an artist's paradise for years and they have never been to the clean, well-scrubbed Polish section in the northeast, where they could eat not only off the floors but the porches.

And they have perhaps never even been to Little Italy, which I think is the most colorful of all. Little Italy, actually, is a street of sidewalk markets running from Wharton to Catharine on Ninth. But the name is a misnomer. The Italians have the fruit and vegetable and dish stands and pushcarts. The Jewish street merchants have the clothing "shops." Positions are often hereditary on this street and it is a place where you are not surprised if a tomato peddler breaks into an operatic aria between shouting his wares and his prices.

It further occurs to me that the town has had many great football players: Penn's Big Bill Hollenback, the late T. Truxtun Hare, Paul Scull, Frank Reagan, Franny Murray, Chuck Bednarik (Philly's greatest contribution to the pros) . . . Temple's Swede Hansen, Dave Smukler, Pete Stevens, Andy Tomasic . . . Villanova's Johny Wysocki, Eddie Michaels, Gene Filipski.

There have also been many great stars, like Jim Thorpe, Bronko Nagurski, Red Grange and Ernie Nevers. But the greatest one I ever saw was that big bull Smukler. When he was at his best, this mighty fullback, Pop Warner's pride during his days of coaching the Owls late in his career, was the finest all-round player I have ever seen in action.

And the most affecting human-interest story I ever heard about a football player involved a Temple man. It was after an Eagles' game at Shibe Park (now Connie Mack Stadium in tribute to the Grand Old Man of Baseball).

Joe Smith, manager of the Wagner Ballroom, was walking into the dressing room to give his regards to guard Piggy Barnes. He met an old friend at the door. Not many years before this old friend had put a college on the football map with his spectacular runs. He had been the first big star of this same Eagles' pro team. But now, on this Sunday in 1949, far from his times of triumph and his fields of glory, he stood at the dressing-room door forgotten and unrecognized by a new crowd of hero worshipers.

He stood there humbly and sheepishly. And almost boyishly—the cycle perhaps complete—he said to Smith, "Say, Joe, you think you could get me into the dressing room? I'd like to meet that Steve Van Buren."

"Sure," Smith said. And an old running star named Swede Hansen went into the dressing room to meet a new one.

It still further occurs to me that:

Nobody has ever lived a more exemplary life and received more laudatory stories than Philadelphia fighter Tommy Loughran, and nobody has gotten into more sensational headline stories than Philadephia fight manager Frank (Blinky) Palermo, who takes more pride in his family than his champions.

Dewey Yesner, the onetime carnival pitch man who built a local empire of hot dog and orange drink stands (Dewey's), was nicknamed for Admiral Dewey but he never got any farther than the Delaware River during the three years he was in the Navy. Dewey, incidentally, has quietly given help to hundreds of men from his old calling when they have been down on their luck.

The two biggest mysteries our town has had were the Judge Crater-like disappearance of Magistrate Jules Forstein's wife and the suicide of Police Inspector Craig Ellis.

Sherman Billingsley is a piker in presenting gifts to customers compared to the way Frankie Palumbo operated when he had the

Click (with the longest bar in the world) and other midtown clubs, before he settled down to fatherhood and a more quiet life.

Philadephians may not be able to tell you what buildings are at some of the historic sites, but to a man and a woman they can tell you what Broad and Locust is known for—the sportsmen. The men, that is, who make and take wagers. On anything from a nag at Tropical to what make car will pass next.

The unique Mayor's Office for Information and Complaints, which was opened in 1952, has an office staff of twelve. It needs that many. It handles some four hundred citizens a day. Some of the complaints are justified. All of them have to be investigated.

You couldn't meet a nicer gentleman than Ron Delany, Villanova's great miler who became an Olympic champ in 1956; or Temple's basketball star Guy Rodgers; or that school's great Hal Lear, who shattered all of those NCAA tourney scoring marks in 1956.

There is something reassuring about the sound of bacon sizzling on the griddle in our all-night diners.

People eating alone in cafeterias late at night seem like the loneliest people in the world—the folks the big town swallowed up and forgot.

If our town wants to raise some revenue in a hurry all it has to do is station a few cops on Chestnut and Walnut streets on Saturday nights. The bag of speeders, hotrodders and reckless drivers will be a big one.

In our town it seems to me:

The best waitresses are never the prettiest ones.

The women who look silly in silly hats wear the silliest ones.

The stout women who work in restaurants and diners always have a tendency to mother their customers.

Many men call lawyers "counselors" when they greet them, and it sounds as phony as it frequently is.

Half of the women drivers look scared to death driving in midtown traffic, and half of the men should be the way they drive.

You're never going to be able to teach women to have change ready when they get on trolleys or buses.

People who don't applaud during a club show seem to have more of a grudge against the world than the acts.

All cabdrivers must have strong constitutions or they would be suffering nervous breakdowns.

Nothing makes a stomach squirm so much as seeing a parent bawl out or berate a child in public, causing that speechless embarrassment only the young can know.

The most outlandish hats are always worn by women who couldn't attract attention any other way.

There is little hope for couples who discuss their personal problems and beliefs loudly enough for everybody else in a bus or trolley to hear.

The most selfish and boorish drivers are those who honk their horns when they are being held up for a few seconds by a funeral procession crossing an intersection against the light.

Redheads are decreasing in number.

Girls should wear a lot of yellow in the springtime.

Movie-goers who eat their candy or popcorn the loudest always get quiet during the unimportant scene in a picture.

Bartenders look furtively disgusted when you ask for any cocktail except a martini or a manhattan.

Magazines in the doctors' and dentists' offices are getting more up to date.

Shoeshine men (including our "Daddy," the old Negro gentleman who has been in front of the Federal Building at Ninth and Market streets for years) rarely have their shoes shined.

The most appealing real life picture I have ever seen in our town was that of a threadbare old guy driving a junk wagon over Filbert Street with his mongrel dog sitting proudly on the seat beside him. They weren't on an old junk wagon, really. They were, with each other, two kings on a throne. They still go around the midtown streets together and one of these days you may be lucky enough to see them. It will make you feel better about everything.

Chapter VI

Pardon Some Boasting about the Town

PHILADELPHIANS are not customarily given to boasting. They will agree with you that "Yes, Philly is sort of a slow town." But the time has come to break the rule and do a little boasting for them.

Let's put it simply and bluntly, people of the nation. Where would the nation be without Philly? A slow town? Well, let's consider a few things. Or a few hundred things.

The quotation "Victory goes to the one who gits there fustest with the mostest" has been ascribed to two Confederate generals, Thomas (Stonewall) Jackson and Nathan Bedford Forrest. There need be no dispute about which city in the country was first or fastest with the mostest. It's Philly—and that's fact.

It has led since colonial days in the man-made developments which ultimately constituted the heart, soul, mind and body of the United States.

It has more firsts and oldests than any other city in the nation, almost as many as the number of traffic tickets given out daily to motorists who casually ignore its NO PARKING signs.

You want historical stuff? We have it in abundance.

Scientific stuff? It's here, and plentiful.

Religious stuff? Cultural? Educational? Entertainment stuff? We have it.

Paraphrasing the old tune, "We got plenty of everything."

And everything starts with history. Let's start with that. Oh yes, and every American life begins with a precious possession called freedom. The two of them, history and freedom, go together here in our big town. That freedom, it began here, down in Independence Hall, in a quiet section of the city over which the spirit of our forefathers still seems to hover on a cold winter night if you stroll past and allow warm, idle thoughts to take you on a walk into another century.

Daytimes you can stop in and see the desk at which the signers affixed their names—John Hancock's largest of all—to the Declaration of Independence, first read to the people on Chestnut Street between Fifth and Sixth on July 8, 1776.

The Constitution under which you live had the same birthplace, its creators concluding their labors on September 17, 1787.

On Chestnut Street, too, are Congress Hall and Carpenters' Hall, scene of many lesser but still significant developments in the birth and growth of a nation.

The first White House was in Philadelphia, at 526–30 Market Street, which now is a shabby, run-down, fading part of the business district, several blocks below the big and modern department stores.

Here, at 239 Arch Street, is the ancient little brick house where Betsy Ross lived and where, tradition and legend have it, she made the first American flag.

The first of Uncle Sam's mints was built here and the First Bank of the United States, chartered in 1791 and constructed at 116 South Third Street six years later.

Thanks mainly to that greatest all-round American, Benjamin Franklin, Philadelphia had:

The first circulating library, begun in 1731, with the first board of directors including Franklin, Thomas Cadwalader and Thomas Hopkinson. The present Free Library of Philadelphia, established in 1891, has its main building on the Benjamin Franklin Parkway at Nineteenth and Vine streets. A $6,500,000 structure opened in 1927, it is one of the largest in the world and in motif resembles the buildings by Gabriel on the Place de la Concorde.

The first social and intellectual club, the Junto. And from this developed the American Philosophical Society, which still meets in the hall it has occupied since 1787.

The first hospital, the Pennsylvania Hospital, founded in 1751.

The first volunteer fire company in the world, started in 1736.

The first fire insurance company, the Philadelphia Contributorship, formed in 1752.

The first art institution, the Pennsylvania Academy of the Fine Arts (and don't forget the second *the*, as too many rewrite men have). Philadelphia has been busy in the world of art ever since. There are the Philadelphia Museum of Art, one of the great ones in the world, impressive and imposing in its majestic building at the head of the Parkway; the Museum School of Art, Penn's School of Fine Arts, the Tyler School of Fine Arts at Temple, the Moore Institute of Art, Science and Industry, the Rodin Museum, the Art Alliance, the Samuel S. Fleisher Art Memorial (formerly the Graphic Sketch Club) and numerous private galleries. The Philadelphia Sketch Club, ninety-five years old, is the oldest art club in the country.

The first university, the University of Pennsylvania, which began with the Charity School in 1740. That ever-active Ben gave it a push, it started to confer degrees and ten years later, when it added a medical school, it became a university.

The Rowbottom, a less praiseworthy aspect of the town's life, also originated here—at Penn. In a Rowbottom students roll on to the streets, halt traffic, plague the police and generally comport themselves in a fashion hardly expected from college men. Whether the outbursts are due to animal or infantile spirits has never been determined.

With Penn as the leader of the parade, Philadelphia has become one of the leading educational centers of the country.

Next to Penn in size and stature is Temple University, which was founded by the Reverend Dr. Russell H. Conwell, who gained a national reputation with his "Acres of Diamonds" (are to be found right in your own backyard) speech. Its college charter was obtained in 1888.

Then, within the city limits, there are those two progressive

Catholic schools, La Salle College (which publishes the town's only literary quarterly, *Four Quarters*) and St. Joseph's College; the Drexel Institute of Technology; Girard College, first orphan college in the country; Dropsie College, a Hebrew institution; and a host of specialized schools, including the renowned Curtis Institute of Music and the first medical institution for women, the Woman's Medical College.

And just outside the city are those two Quaker schools with such excellent reputations and high scholastic standards, Haverford and Swarthmore Colleges; Villanova University; Bryn Mawr College, one of the most famous for women; Beaver College, another well-known learning spot for girls; and Chestnut Hill and Rosemont Colleges, still others for the young lady. Farther from town, but in the metropolitan area, are West Chester State Teachers College and Lincoln University, the Negro school.

Philadelphia also has the only high school in the nation empowered to confer degrees, Central High, which opened in 1838.

It had the first parochial high school in the land, the Roman Catholic High School, endowed in 1878 by a bequest from Thomas E. Cahill. All of its Quaker schools date back many years. Penn Charter, the oldest, was founded in 1689.

It had the first Officers' Candidate School, one established at 1210 Chestnut Street during the Civil War. The first Negro company in the Union Army was mustered at this spot in 1863.

The town also has the oldest zoo in America at Thirty-fourth Street and Girard Avenue in rambling, rolling Fairmount Park. The Zoological Society of Philadelphia, which sponsored it, was incorporated in 1859 and the zoo opened in 1874.

Long before that, about 1728, pioneer botanist John Bartram (David Rittenhouse, the first American astronomer, also lived in town) began the first botanic garden in the country along the Schuylkill. There is little left of Bartram's Gardens but the house which he built himself was restored by the Fairmount Park Commission.

There are some other historic houses in the town, too, in addition to those of Miss Ross and Mr. Bartram.

The Morris House at 5442 Germantown Avenue, built by a merchant named David Deschler in 1772, was the headquarters of British army commander Sir William Howe after the Battle of Germantown. The Stenton Mansion at Eighteenth and Courtland streets was built in 1728 by Penn's aide, James Logan. And there are many others, quaint and picturesque, through the slopes of Fairmount Park.

There are absolutely no Philadelphians, I venture to say, who are not acquainted with the scenic delights of this Park. But there are many citizens, I am certain, who are unaware of the historic associations provided by those houses, which spring up from the green loam of the "country" within a city from time to time.

The Letitia Street House, for instance, is a plain little two-story dwelling. But it's a real oldie. Once known as the William Penn House, it was thought to have been built by the founder. That turned out to be wrong. The house wasn't even constructed until sometime between 1703 and 1715. Originally it was on Letitia Street, named for Penn's daughter. That street down by the Delaware River in time was surrounded by buildings reflecting the growing town, and the house was removed to Fairmount Park in 1883.

Lemon Hill on the East River Drive was once the site of the country seat of Robert Morris, the financier of the Revolution. Morris, of course, subsequently ran into financial troubles of his own and the estate was sold by the sheriff in 1799 after Morris had been tossed into prison for debts. Morris' home, no longer around, stood northeast of the present Lemon Hill Mansion.

The Belmont Mansion, just north of the town's Horticultural Hall and one of the best known to the natives, was originally built by a gentleman named William Peters in 1742 and was the scene of elegant parties attended by leading American figures during the Revolutionary War days and the first years of the nation's official life. The mansion was acquired by the city in 1867 and it, like the Letitia Street House, was restored by the Philadelphia Museum of Art.

Little known to the townspeople are the Ormiston and Randolph mansions. The Randolph Mansion was bought by Dr. Philip Syng Physick, "the father of American surgery" and first professor of surgery at the University of Pennsylvania, in 1828 for his daughter, Mrs. Randolph, and thereby acquired its present name. But it dates back to colonial days.

Ormiston has a less happy background. It was the estate of Joseph Galloway, the most hated Tory of his day. As a matter of fact, the state confiscated the property in 1778 and sold it to a good soldier for the revolutionary cause, General Joseph Reed.

The Solitude Mansion, which is within the zoo grounds, was built in 1784 by John Penn, a grandson of the founder. Sweetbrier Mansion, built by Samuel Breck, dates back to 1797. Older than that is Lansdowne Mansion, built about 1773 by John Penn, cousin of the founder and last of the provincial governors.

Predating the Lansdowne Mansion is Mt. Pleasant Mansion, which probably contains more history than any of them. Lying west of the Columbia Avenue entrance to the park, it was built about 1761 by a Captain John Macpherson, who made his fortune as a privateer during the French and Indian War. It was purchased by General Benedict Arnold in 1779, before he had become a traitor. Arnold bought it as a wedding present for the girl he intended to marry, pretty Peggy Shippen. When he betrayed the people of his country, the state stepped in and seized the estate. For a time the home was leased by Baron von Steuben, the drillmaster hero of the Continental Army.

All of this is not information that could be furnished by any citizen you might meet walking down the street. Most citizens wouldn't have the slightest idea about where most of these historic houses are, and would not be able to identify them when they saw them. There are many citizens, no doubt, who have not visited most of the historical shrines. There are some, very probably, who have never been inside Independence Hall.

A young soldier not too long ago told me a story which typifies this. He had come home from camp on a week-end pass and he had brought along two buddies who were in training with him and wanted to see their alma mater, the University of North Carolina, in the Eastern regional play of the NCAA basketball tournament. They watched the game on Friday night and after it was over—since the next one wouldn't be until the following night—suggested that a tour of Philadelphia's historic shrines would be in order on Saturday.

Would the local boy consent to be their guide for the tour, they asked.

Filled with pride in his home town and its glorious past, the young soldier quickly agreed. And then the realization came to him suddenly that he didn't know where some of the shrines were, because he himself had never visited them. He never confessed to his buddies. He looked up the addresses and read up on some of the necessary information and, when he served as their guide, he acted quite knowing and casual about the whole business. But when he took his visiting friends to the Betsy Ross House and old Christ Church burial ground, he was also seeing those places for the first time.

Come to think about it, there are probably a host of Philadelphians who don't know how their city got its name. So perhaps that should be put on the record right now.

Penn named his city after one in Lydia, Asia Minor. The word comes from the Greek and it means "brotherly love," which perhaps is something else that many of the citizens don't know.

The site of our town still had the Indian name of Coaquanock when Penn landed in 1682. There had been a Swedish settlement on the site earlier but nothing much happened until King Charles II gave the land to Penn.

As a fellow named Gabriel Thomas wrote to a friend some fifteen years later:

"Since that time [when Penn arrived], the industrious inhabitants have built a nobel and beautiful city, and called it Philadelphia, or Brotherly Love, which contains a number of houses, all inhabited; and most of them stately; and of brick.

"This city is situated between Schoolkillriver and the great river Delaware, which derives its name from Captain Delaware, who came there pretty early; ships of two or three hundred tons may come up to the city, by either of these two rivers."

Ships have been coming up the Delaware at an increasing rate ever since and Penn's town has become the largest fresh-water port in the world. It lies eighty-eight nautical miles from the sea but it is second only to New York in total business. By 1956 a cargo ship was landing or leaving every half-hour around the clock and there were some 250 regular sailings every month. Along the

Delaware were 267 piers and wharves to handle every type of marine commerce, 41 of them water-front terminals for three great railroads—the Pennsylvania, the Baltimore & Ohio and the Reading. In 1956 the port handled 39,697,692 tons of import commerce—an all-time high. It has been the nation's top import port since 1954. Export tonnage in 1956 was 6,071,088 tons.

Oh yes, and getting back to houses after all this time, there are some others you shouldn't miss and you have to stroll down toward the Delaware to find them. They are on one of the most interesting and fascinating streets in the United States. It lies between Arch and Race and Front and Second streets and is called Elfreth's Alley. And it has quite a claim to fame and permanence. It is the oldest continuously inhabited street in the entire Western Hemisphere.

No other street in our land can make that statement.

Somewhere in any book about Philadelphia there should appear the prayer which William Penn wrote for his town. This seems the proper chapter. Penn wrote the prayer in 1684. It can be found inscribed on a plaque in City Hall Plaza:

"And thou Philadelphia, the virgin settlement of this province named before thou wert born, what love, what care, what service and what travail has there been to bring thee forth and preserve thee from such as would abuse and defile thee. O that thou mayest be kept from the evil that would overwhelm thee, that faithful to the God of thy mercies, in the Life of righteousness, thou mayest be preserved to the end. My soul prays to God for thee that thou mayest stand in the day of trial, that thy children may be blest of the Lord, and thy people saved by His power."

Philadelphia has been called the City of Churches, as well as the City of Homes and the City of Brotherly Love—and not without good reason. For its 495,207 dwelling places (in all, the city had some 545,000 buildings at last count), it has more than 1,300 churches. These include:

The famous Christ Church on Second Street above Market, founded in 1695 under the terms of a clause in Penn's charter from King Charles II. Its present building was constructed between 1727 and 1754, fifteen signers of the Declaration of Independence worshiped at the church and seven lie buried in its three burial grounds.

Gloria Dei (Old Swedes') Church at Swanson and Christian streets, the oldest house of worship in Pennsylvania. Its congregation was formed in 1642, the first services on the site were held in a log blockhouse built in 1669. Among those buried in its churchyard are Alexander Wilson, father of American ornithology, and Gustavus Hesselius, first American portrait painter.

Old St. George's M. E. Church, the oldest church building owned and used by Methodists anywhere in the world. Located at Fourth Street above Race, it was built for a German reformed congregation in 1763 and bought by the Methodists six years later.

Old St. Joseph's Church on Willings Alley east of Fourth Street, which was the first Roman Catholic church in the city.

St. Thomas P. E. Church, oldest church congregation organized by Negroes in this country.

Synagogue of Mikveh Israel, first Jewish congregation in Philadelphia. The present building was dedicated in 1828.

Pennypack Baptist Church in Bustleton. The present building, erected in 1805, is the place of worship for the oldest congregation of this denomination in the city, founded in 1688.

St. Peter's Church at Third and Pine streets, where services were first held in 1761. It is famed for its boys' choir.

Old St. Mary's, founded in 1763 and first cathedral in the city. It is on Fourth Street above Spruce.

"Old Pine" Presbyterian at Fourth and Pine streets, which was the only Presbyterian building in colonial Philadelphia. Its date of origin is 1764.

St. Michael's Lutheran Church, which was the denomination's first here. Its building, torn down in 1872, was the largest church in North America when it was built.

Philadelphia also had a now-forgotten gentleman named Joshua Humphreys, who is considered to be the father of our Navy, a ship architect who believed in speed and produced the frigate.

In 1842 the first suspension bridge of any type was built here on the present site of the Spring Garden Street Bridge.

The first railroad operated here in 1809, being constructed by one Thomas Leiper to haul stone from the Delaware to Crum Creek. The cars were hauled along the tracks by horses. Some decades passed and it was then time for the city to turn out the first train hauled by a locomotive, an engine with wooden wheels dubbed "Old Ironsides" and built at the old Baldwin Works in 1832. It operated over the Philadelphia, Germantown and Norristown Railway.

The first iron bridge ever built can be claimed by West Manayunk.

Philadelphia can be proud of the fact that the oldest active military organization in the nation was formed here. It is the First City Troop, organized in 1774 and now the Reconnaissance Company, 28th Infantry, Pennsylvania National Guard. Originally cavalry and first called the Light Horse of the City of Philadelphia, it was established by twenty-eight young men simply because it looked as though there was going to be a war with England. They volunteered their services to the Continental Congress and have been engaged in every American conflict.

The first building and loan association was established in the town in 1831 at what is now 4217–21 Frankford Avenue. A lamplighter received the first loan. He wanted to build a house on Orchard Street. William Penn would have liked that.

"Home Sweet Home" was given its first airing here some 158 years ago at a theater called, of all things, the Prune Street Theater.

And that's not all.

This is supposed to be a sleepy town, too. Not much doing. But for a sleepy town it seems to have gotten a host of things started so far as the happy world of entertainment is concerned.

Consider these facts:

On November 21, 1766, the first theater in America was opened in Philadelphia. It was the Southwark and it was located at South and Apollo streets, which is now the oldest Negro section of our town.

The first American play, *The Prince of Parthia* by Thomas Godfrey, Jr., was produced here on April 23, 1767.

The Walnut Street Theater, built in 1809, is not only the oldest playhouse in America, it is among the oldest in the world devoted to the drama. It is still standing, it hasn't missed a season and the acoustics remain the best of any theater in the town.

The second oldest playhouse in the country was also located here. It was the Arch Street Theater, managed for some thirty years by Mrs. John Drew, who was the grandmother of Ethel, Lionel and John Barrymore.

As a matter of fact, stage activities in this country began in Philadelphia—first Shakespearean productions, first puppet show, first minstrel shows—and the town has continued to keep a heady pace.

The Savoy Company, which staged its fifty-fourth annual production in 1957, is the oldest nonprofessional Gilbert and Sullivan group in continuous existence.

Philadelphia, of course, doesn't have the legitimate theater attractions that New York presents. But it has become a beehive of little theater activity since the Hedgerow Theater out Moylan way became a nationally known group.

And in its Playhouse in the Park (Fairmount, naturally) it has the first municipally owned and operated summer tent theater. Six years old in the summer of 1957, it is the particular hobby of onetime bricklayer John B. Kelly, along with the Atlantic City Race Track.

Robin Hood Dell, the music ampitheater for summer concerts in the park (Fairmount, naturally), has had twenty-eight seasons. It's the pet project of City Representative Fredric R. Mann, who is also a box manufacturer and a piano player.

The town hasn't neglected the movies either. One of the first film studios was the Lubin Studios, opened in 1898 by an optician named Sigmund Lubin. This motion-picture pioneer a year later opened at Seventh and Market streets what was very probably the first movie theater in the country.

The first dance band remote was aired in Philly in June of 1922 when radio station WIP broadcast the music of Charlie Kerr and his orchestra from the Cafe L'Aiglon. The town was the center of live dance music for radio listeners for years after that.

Philadelphia has the oldest ballroom and academy in America.

It is the Wagner Ballroom, which was founded by "Professor" Wagner at 44 N. Fourth Street in 1893, and is now being operated by the third generation of his family. Thousands of natives learned their dance steps at this spot through the years. Back in 1920 there were as many as forty teachers, but now—in its new site at 5810 Old York Road—it's mostly for dancing.

Primarily the dancers are young but that certainly doesn't apply to one Harry L. Gormley. A retired Army officer and a West Point graduate, he was still reporting for action in 1957 at the age of eighty-seven. He started dancing at Wagner's in 1903 and in recent years he had to limit his activities to Saturday nights. But early this year he was still arriving every Saturday night to take a seat in the corner by the bandstand, listen and watch, dance a few numbers himself, and then be driven home.

Now, let's see——

Well, the first political cartoon in America appeared in the Pennsylvania *Gazette*. The year was 1754.

Philadelphia is also the home of the first and oldest advertising agency in the country, N. W. Ayer & Son. A vice president of the organization, former newspaperman Richard Powell, properly enough, wrote the best-selling novel called *The Philadelphian.*

The agency follows a traditional line and I remember that when a friend of mine, Roddy Rogers, who had been a director for WFIL-TV, was offered a job with Ayer, he asked his father about the advisability of accepting. His father happens to be a likable socialite named Edmund Rogers, who has his own firm in town, Gray & Rogers.

Said the elder Rogers:

"As long as there is advertising, there is Ayer."

Roddy took the job. The line became well known in the trade.

Both the first ice cream and the first ice-cream sodas were made in Philadelphia. At one time ice-cream hawkers went along the streets with their cans of ice cream, pushing them in barrows, and they were called "hokey pokey men."

The street merchants in the past also included oyster vendors (wares sold only before noontime), "whitey wash men" (who cleaned out cellars), pie men and umbrella men.

About the only ones remaining are the pretzel men, who sell those big doughy pretzels on which gobs of mustard are to be applied. From time to time the city has tried to get rid of them on the ground that the whole business is unsanitary. But the natives have kept on patronizing the pretzel vendors. They like old things, including doughy pretzels. And there is hardly anybody who ever went to high school or college in the town who hasn't found, at one time or another, that a big doughy pretzel—with mustard—makes quite a satisfactory lunch.

Oh yes, and Philadelphia, in addition to having the first medical school, also had the first law school, the first dental school, the first pharmacy schoool, and . . .

But you get the general idea.

Chapter VII

It's an Old Quaker City Custom

THE APPEARANCE of William Penn's "green countrie towne" has been changing greatly in recent years.

Billy Penn's big city wears a New Look. From head to toe it's displaying a fancy new collection of structural raiment—from the Presidential Apartments and the other new modernistic buildings on City Line, pushing the open country still farther west, through all of the public and private housing projects here and there and everywhere, into the strikingly attractive Penn Center in the midtown, and on down to the new International Airport.

There are, in addition to all of the new homes within the city limits—and the many more in all of the quick-rising suburban developments—new playgrounds, new office buildings, new police and fire stations and new shopping centers. And there will be more changes in this congested, slow-moving city which finally decided to do something about its problems and acted quickly, sometimes too quickly, once the program began—because at times in recent months it seemed as though almost every street was being dug up for one reason or another.

As the year 1957 began 10,000 acres of Philadelphia were being transformed and rejuvenated. Some eighteen major redevelopment projects were under way. Among these were Penn Center, bringing a new vista of skyline to the midtown; the expressway system (the Schuylkill and Delaware expressways, the Walt Whitman Bridge and all connecting links), changing the roads and the routes for millions of motorists; the Independence Mall, including Independence Historic Park, bringing scenic beauty as well as historical significance to the well-known shrines; the 400-acre Food Distribution Center in the southeastern section, conceived by the Greater Philadelphia Movement; and the preparation of 3,000 acres of meadows in Eastwick for home and industry.

The projects around Independence Hall had given impetus to private enterprise in that area and the result was a rehabilitation of the old Society Hill section, once the elite residential district. Even the Mayor was building a brand-new home there.

But with all of the changes, many traditional things were totally untouched. Some of them were important, some were trivial. But they all helped to add up to the atmosphere that provides Philadelphia with more of its small-town flavor.

Philadelphians do not change easily, or quickly. Nor are they particularly anxious for changes in the city or its customs or its way of life. If changes must come, changes like the Penn Center, the expressways, the Independence Mall, so be it. It's fine. But Philadelphians do not get particularly excited about changes nor do they, except for city officials and the Chamber of Commerce, boast about changes or progress.

They are modest souls. And they are also to an emphatic extent creatures of habit. They tend to shop on the same day or night year after year, go to the theater on the same night of the week and eat at the same dining places they have patronized for decades. They also tend to work at one place and stick at one job. They like an air of permanency about them.

All of this perhaps was typified in a little incident which occurred early in 1957 when the old Philadelphia importing firm of John Wagner & Sons, Inc., down at 233 Dock Street moved out to Hatboro. On their last day at the old stand three members of the firm—Ralph Starr, Charles Sinkler and Norwood Weaver—

went to Old Original Bookbinders, the nationally known sea-food house nearby, for lunch.

The restaurant's general manager, Joseph Donnolo, was familiar with the fact that the company was moving. Casually he asked the three men: "When were you founded?"

"Eighteen forty-seven," he was told. "When were *you* founded?"

"Eighteen-sixty-three," he said.

One of the waitresses, Martha Rentz, was standing near the table to take the order. "Where," she asked the men, "did you people eat between 1847 and 1863?"

That tells the story pretty well. Philadelphians like the old things, the old way of doing things.

The PTC under its new owners introduced many changes—most tending to modernize the transit system, but not all for the better—and in January, 1957, it placed into service the one thousandth new bus since its program began in April 1955. But many riders didn't like the modernization. Many still preferred the trolleys that have vanished completely from other cities, and regularly they wrote letters to the newspapers to say so.

Even entertainers, the pianist-singers, the plain piano players, seem to stay in one club or musical bar or hotel room for long periods extending into years in our town.

And retirement parties for men or women who have been working for one company or in one store for forty-five, fifty, sixty years are held by the scores every year.

Undoubtedly the most famous example of that kind of longevity was the tall, lean Connie Mack, who was at the helm of the Athletics for almost half a century—from 1901 to 1950—while entirely new generations of managers came along to be hired and fired and rehired and fired again.

In their work or their hobbies or their social affairs, Philadelphians like the comfort of an old shoe. Mack's story is the best known but there are many others.

There are many things that never seem to change in our town, certain things you can always expect.

You expect a host of elderly couples to have lunch in Wanamaker's tea room when they come into the midtown. They wouldn't think of going anywhere else.

You expect that a host of society people from the inherit-the-money and clip-the-coupons Main Line would have their parties and special affairs nowhere but at the Barclay on Rittenhouse Square.

You expect thousands of people with less cash to have their quick lunch nowhere but at a Horn & Hardart automat or a Linton's restaurant.

You can expect scrapple for breakfast, pepper pot soup for lunch and ice cream for dessert.

You can also expect a lot of people to have a cinnamon bun, another local creation, for breakfast.

If a big fight is staged in town, Herman (Muggsy) Taylor, an experienced old hand at the job, will be the promoter.

Frank (Blinky) Palermo, you can almost expect, will be in a corner as the manager of one of the fighters, the feeble efforts by the State Athletic Commission to take away the license of the always sorely troubled, in-a-jam but happy-go-lucky Blink having failed.

Dave Zinkoff, known by one and all as "the Zink," once the campus cutup at Temple University back in the early 30s, will be making the announcements at the sports events in the Arena and Convention Hall.

The automobiles will be rolling over the Delaware River Bridge for the shore points by the thousands on Friday and Saturday and coming back over clogged highways that enforce a snail-like pace on Sunday night.

The people will go to the resorts to which they have always gone —Atlantic City for the classy hotels, Ocean City for the family homes (that's where the Kelly clan goes, incidentally), Cape May for the family tradition, Wildwood for the plentiful clubs.

BRIDGE TRAFFIC RECORDS BROKEN, the Monday morning headline will read.

Having been booed unmercifully for striking out on his last appearance at the plate, a Phillies' player will hit a home run. He will be loudly applauded when he completes the circuit.

St. Joseph's College will have the most vociferous rooters at the college basketball games in Penn's Palestra.

Some of the Mummers will be obviously drunk as they parade up Broad Street.

The same powerful men will dine in the Union League, stronghold and to some extent symbol of the Republican party ever since Lincoln's day. The names of the men will change but their faces somehow remain alike through the years. And it is that way, too, with their confident manner, their bearing of assurance that all's right with the world—at least within their own sturdy, impregnable walls.

Members of the 32-Carat Club will have some of the rowdiest verbal fun you have ever heard at their meetings while planning a number of good deeds for the month.

At least one private club will be raided early Sunday morning.

At least three Negro homes will be raided as disorderly houses for serving liquor illegally.

There will be talk that another club is going to fold.

Plans to improve Traffic Court will be announced.

And even if it's freezing cold, thousands of Philadelphians will take their children into the central city streets and stand on tiptoes or sit on the traditional peach baskets or gawk from high hotel windows to watch the annual Mummers Parade on New Year's Day. . . . To see the appearance of the fancy divisions with their bright and gaudy costumes, the jockeys with their wide-flowing capes, the comic divisions with their lampooning (often in the broadest of strokes) of current events and headline figures of the moment, the string bands (Ferko, Uptown, and all the others) with their familiar and infectious rhythms. Formerly neither rain nor snow nor sleet stayed them from their appointed rounds. And the outpouring of the mobs to see them in all kinds of weather was a part of the spirit of the occasion.

Never, in the old days, was a New Year's Day welcomed without the air being filled with the strains of "Oh, Dem Golden Slippers," traditional theme of the string bands with all of their banjos strumming. Now the parade is postponed, pushed back, if the rain is heavy or the snow is falling, in order that the costumes, the work of many months and considerable expense, are not spoiled and the crowd does not diminish in numbers. Or perhaps it is because this is a more businesslike era in which we live, as well as one in which a high premium is placed on creature comforts.

The old mummers—or shooters—were a hardy lot, and the old citizens who watched them for decades were hardier, too. Nonetheless, this annual outpouring of shooters from South Philly (home section of the mummers for many years) and all about the town to parade up Broad Street in a panorama of color, music and fun, the men in costume cavorting across the wide street in that mincing strut which is half march step and half dance, remains to the city what the annual stop of the circus or carnival or county fair has always been to the small town.

The shooters go back a long time. They go back to the town's first days, actually, when young scamps would don silly costumes and go reveling through the streets around Christmas time asking for penny donations. Sometimes they shot off firecrackers, thus prompting the name which has stuck to this day. For many years the parades were strictly neighborhood affairs. Then, in 1876, the mummers marched to Independence Hall and other sections in individual groups. And finally, in 1901, the present pattern was established. That was the first city-wide parade, in which the mummers snaked their way up Broad Street and prizes were offered by City Hall, thanks to those politically powerful contractors, the Vare brothers, Edward and William.

In 1957 the parade made network television for the first time, which could mean that it has finally arrived as a national spectacle. The chances are, however, that it will never reach the status of a New Orleans Mardi Gras, which is a festive occasion as well as a spectacle; or even the Tournament of Roses parade in Pasadena, California, which is certainly a prettier sight.

But Philadelphians have loved it for many years and, even when they know or can anticipate what's going to be in it, love it still. And if a hydrogen bomb doesn't hit, they'll be bundling up their children and taking them into the midtown to see it centuries hence. And the tune will still be "Oh, Dem Golden Slippers." You can bet on that.

Unless the bomb hits, you can be certain, too, that on Friday afternoons some limousines, big and long and black, always chauffeur-driven and frequently old-fashioned, will roll up to the front of the Academy of Music and deposit some gray-haired old ladies from some old families at the door for the Philadelphia Orchestra concerts.

It's been that way for many decades now and if the Mummers Parade is the town's big carnival affair, its biggest cultural tradition is the Academy, that grand Old Lady of Broad Street, which was opened on January 26, 1857, has lived an impressive and stately century, and is currently undergoing renovations aimed at removing some of the signs of old age from its weather-beaten countenance. The work is being done under the planning and execution of a nonprofit corporation headed by appliance distributor Stuart F. Loucheim.

This cultural shrine, an imposing but grimy building with poor heating and plumbing as it reached its centennial year, was constructed with many of the designs and features of the famous La Scala opera house in Milan, Italy, and its acoustics are considered second only to those of that music temple today.

Aside from that consideration, it is estimated by architects that a new building seating the same number of spectators would cost close to $25,000,000, reason enough for restoration rather than starting all over from scratch. But the old town would never have been the same with a brand-new Academy, as it would most certainly never be the same without the distinguished Philadelphia Orchestra, one of the half-dozen greatest ones in the world, perhaps the greatest.

Nor would it look the same without the familiar figure of conductor Eugene Ormandy, who followed the more temperamental Leopold Stokowski to the podium and, in typical Philadelphia fashion, has been at the one job in the one place for a long time.

The orchestra nabobs began to have trouble with the perennially youthful Stokowski in 1931 and from that year until 1935 Ormandy was a guest conductor. From 1936 to 1940 he served as co-conductor. He has been the sole boss since 1941.

The Academy has been operated smoothly for years now under the commanding hand of its treasurer and manager, Harold T. Mason. And this is probably the place to mention also Emma Feldman, the veteran feminine impresario who has promoted so many special concerts at the Academy; and well-liked Bill Huff, who handled the Philadelphia Forum programs for so many years.

Not all Philadelphians are classical music lovers. Thousands who have never seen the orchestra have been in its home only to watch Louis (Satchmo) Armstrong and other jazz greats heat up the staid premises from time to time. But all Philadelphians are proud of the orchestra and its world renown. It is one thing they might even boast about.

Society, of course, quickly took the Academy and the orchestra under its wing and has always played a vital role, both with cash outlay and moral support, in the operations of the orchestra. Among those still attending the concerts and giving her enthusiastic support to the orchestra as the Academy had its centennial birthday was Mrs. William Woodward Arnett, who has had a considerable number of birthdays herself. As the Academy hit one hundred, she was ninety-three and she had been active with the Orchestra Women's Committee for most of those years. Her first trip to the Academy was in 1884 to attend the charity ball. In those early years the ultraexclusive assembly ball was also held at the Academy.

Mrs. Nicholas G. Roosevelt, who calls the Academy her "second home," has sat in the same seat (No. 12) in the same box for the Friday afternoon concerts for more than half a century.

Miss Frances A. Wister, who was called the "watch lady" of the orchestra (she gave out gold watches for service), had labored in its behalf for decades. She died not too long before the jubilee concert and the lavish party which followed in the new Sheraton Hotel, and many were almost disappointed that her ghost did not appear to make sure that everything was going all right.

The boxholders for that jubilee concert marking the Academy's birthday—Dinah Shore and Danny Kaye providing the common touch—constituted a cross section of leading Philadelphians (and not all from the *Social Register*, I hasten to add) in many fields. Here they are:

Mr. and Mrs. Roosevelt, Mr. and Mrs. Francis Boyer, Mr. and Mrs. Harleston R. Wood, Mr. and Mrs. James Fentress, Mr. and Mrs. Lessing J. Rosenwald, Mr. and Mrs. J. Howard Pew, Mr. and Mrs. Percival E. Foerderer, Mrs. E. Florens Rivinus, Mr.

and Mrs. David Van Pelt, Mr. and Mrs. James P. Magill, Mr. and Mrs. Isaac H. Clothier, Jr., Mr. and Mrs. C. Jared Ingersoll, Mr. and Mrs. Martin W. Clement, Mr. and Mrs. James M. Symes, Mr. and Mrs. Matthew H. McCloskey, Mr. and Mrs. Walter H. Annenberg, Mr. and Mrs. Loucheim, Mr. and Mrs. Wilfred D. Gillen, Mr. and Mrs. Herbert C. Morris, Mrs. John Wintersteen, Mr. Henry P. McIlhenny, Mr. and Mrs. C. Wanton Balis, Jr., Mr. and Mrs. Crawford H. Greenewalt, Mr. and Mrs. J. Bruce Bredin, Mr. and Mrs. Albert M. Greenfield, Mrs. William T. Tonner, Mr. and Mrs. Robert McLean, Mr. and Mrs. Henry W. Breyer, Jr., Mr. and Mrs. George Friedland, Mr. and Mrs. Harry M. Buten, Mr. and Mrs. Philip Klein, Mr. and Mrs. J. Maurice Gray, Mr. and Mrs. Samuel Cooke, Mr. and Mrs. Frederic R. Mann, Mrs. Siegfried Roebling, Mr. and Mrs. John C. Atwood, Jr., Mr. and Mrs. Lloyd C. Carswell, Mr. and Mrs. David Kaplan, and Mr. and Mrs. William Coxe Wright.

That's a lot of money, ladies and gentlemen.

Chapter VIII

More Traditions in the Town

THERE are equally traditional institutions in the town which don't affect a couple of million Philadelphians at all.

The Academy, after all, is a well-loved second home for music lovers of all shapes, sizes and species.

The Mummers Parade is a show for the masses, for all the Joe Doakeses and all their kids.

The Assembly Ball, the Philadelphia Club, the Fish House and the First City Troop are strictly limited to a precious few, whose blood is blue.

Founded in 1732, the Fish House has admitted fewer than two new members a year since that time. Known originally as the State in Schuylkill, this social-dining society moved from its original river mansion site above Fairmount Dam in 1822, has wandered since and is now located on another river, the Delaware, up near Andalusia. Most Philadelphians have never even heard of it. More of them, however, have heard vaguely about what is possibly its best-known contribution to the world—Fish House punch.

Here's the recipe:

Two bottles of rum, old and potent. A bottle of brandy, old

and potent. A quart of water. Three quarters of a pound of sugar to each bottle. A wine glass of peach brandy to each bottle. Three quarters of a quart of lemon juice. The sugar (it has to be lump sugar) goes into the bowl first. The water is then poured in and the sugar stirred into a syrup. After that the lemon juice is added. And finally the potent liquids.

Here's a warning: It's dynamite.

The Philadelphia Club is a little better known to a few more natives, but it isn't as familiar as, say, the Troc—the burlesque theater in town. This club came along later (1834) but it's almost as exclusive as the Fish House. The membership is limited to 435.

This "oldest gentlemen's town club in America" is now primarily a luncheon spot for its aristocratic members who live in the suburban country these days and do not have as much time for the whist or billiards that once occupied them nighttimes in the club quarters at Thirteenth and Walnut streets.

Many more Philadelphians are familiar with the sight, if not the history, of the First City Troop. These present-day soldiers of an organization with a most historic military past still don their colorful full-dress regalia and mount their horses for traditional occasions, the horses sounding echoes from colonial days as they cloppety-clop over the brick streets in the midtown. And passing motorists and pedestrians stop to look and gawk—and wonder what it's all about.

The First City Troop is an hereditary organization, as is the Philadelphia Assembly. Originally invitations to the ultrafashionable assembly balls were rigidly limited to descendants of the founders—and the ball dates back to 1749. But all of these society groups are known only to a small minority.

That would not be true of still another local institution. Everybody knows about Willow Grove Park. It's the only amusement park left for the town, Woodside Park within the city limits having given up the ghost a few years ago. And almost everybody has been there.

This old world and our ways of life have changed considerably with the sometimes meandering march of progress across the passing years, and some of those changes have been reflected quietly in Willow Grove Park, which was sixty-two years old in July, 1957. The world moved more slowly in the departed decades of Willow Grove's youth, people pursued their fun with less speed and more decorum, the family was a more solid social group, manners were more sedate, Paul Whiteman hadn't made a lady out of jazz and that music was still a woman of the New Orleans streets. And, as the old-timers in the audience will know, it was as though all of the summer days and evenings hummed a gentler song.

Tom Houpt was thinking about this one afternoon, and for a little while he was a man caught up in the past with a wistful smile for his own vanished youth. He is a big, gray-haired fellow of fifty-eight whose entire life pretty much revolved around that sprawling playground just out the road a piece from town, and he was remembering because it had just had a birthday and because it was way back in 1914 that he started work at Willow Grove.

Tom Houpt, born in the hamlet of Dreshertown just three miles from the park, was the general superintendent until his retirement in the summer of 1957. But in 1914 he was the program boy.

"I stood at the tunnel where the trolleys came in from all sections of Philadelphia, and Hatboro and Doylestown, too," he recalled, "and I gave out the programs for the band concerts.

"They were different type crowds than you have today. The people came in by trolley—summer trolleys they were—and they made a day of it. Now there is a crowd turnover about three times a day. That's because of the automobile, of course.

"People in those days came as families. The teen-agers come alone now, but in those early days most of them weren't allowed to go out by themselves. Families would almost all bring picnic lunches and sometimes there were excursions all the way from Williamsport. They would have to leave Williamsport at midnight and would reach Willow Grove by 9 A.M.

"The people were better dressed, too. More conservative, that is. You weren't even allowed in the music pavilion unless you had a tie and coat on. And a guard was stationed at each row and

The Mummers

if you talked, he'd tap you on the shoulder and warn you to keep quiet."

The oldest ride at Willow Grove is the Little Scenic, first built in 1896.

"In the early days," Houpt said, "the slow, panoramic rides were the most popular. Then, as the automobile came in, the people wanted more speed, faster rides.

"But the Little Scenic—it used to be called the Nickel Scenic—is still the biggest favorite. It's always been for both young and old."

The outstanding conductors at Willow Grove have included John Philip Sousa, Victor Herbert, Walter Damrosch, Arthur Pryor and Giuseppe Creatore, last member of the big ones, who was creative until his death in 1952 at the age of eighty-two.

"Sousa was there for seventy-eight straight days in 1924," Houpt recalled. "And starting in 1901, he played for twenty-three years. All of the orchestras had to have fifty men and the park was very strict about that. Guards counted the men and sent in daily reports. Sousa received a thousand dollars a day for him and his fifty men. That was for four concerts each day.

"Pryor was a trombonist with Sousa at the beginning. Victor Herbert, I remember, made a big hit with 'Over There.'

"The people loved that. They'd go crazy when he played it. I guess everybody wanted to win the war when they heard it.

"Creatore was the most colorful director. He never used a score."

Willow Grove had one of the first movie houses, built around 1899.

"I remember seeing John Bunny, Flora Finch and Broncho Bill Anderson in the first films we had," Houpt said. "I was the sound effects man then. I was behind the screen and I'd watch the picture and make the noises to fit the scene.

"For shooting I used whips that I'd tap sharply against a leather cushion. For falling water we had a big dishpan with BB's in it. And we had coconut shells to make the sound of horses galloping.

"It seems like a long time ago. . . ."

It was.

And who in the town, in all of those years, has never been there?

Every once in a while it is good to contemplate the good old days when drivers were courteous, kids went barefooted and worried only about nails, there were swimming holes rather than swimming pools, and Babe Ruth and his hot dogs could make front-page headlines.

A Philadelphian named Ben Cantwell was contemplating the old days one time and he wanted to know if I remembered:

Bleacher seats at the ball games for a quarter . . . Green's Hotel . . . The Colonnade . . . The old L'Aiglon . . . John R. K. Scott's coach-and-four . . . Frank Dumont's minstrel troupe, with Charlie Boyden, Eddie Cassidy, Ben Franklin (a later one), Joe Hortese, John Connally and many others . . . W. C. Fields around Nick Hayes' at Broad and Erie. . . .

The circus parades on Germantown Avenue on Monday mornings of the week the show opened . . . School kids shouting gaily because they had been dismissed at 10:30 A.M. to watch . . . Eddie Dowling, Raymond Hitchcock, Kate Smith and Bing Crosby, all playing the Carman when it was a vaudeville theater, during the ownership regime of George Gravenstine and Frank Ackley. . . .

Ty Cobb, Tris Speaker and Al Simmons playing the outfield for the Athletics at the same time . . . Buffalo Bill Cody standing outside his show grounds at Nineteenth Street and Hunting Park Avenue . . . The Indians sitting on the fire escapes of the Park Avenue (this Park Avenue is *not* like New York's Park Avenue) side of the building when the old Convention Hall was at Broad and Allegheny and the Wild West shows and circuses played there . . . Billy Sunday was there once, too. . . .

The steady lead by the sports scribe who covered the Monday night fights at the Olympia: "Lefty Lew Tendler finished his opponent with a left to the solar plexus. . . ." The Frankford Yellow Jackets playing the Canton Bulldogs—with Jim Thorpe, Guyon and Calac in the lineup for the Indians . . . Heinie Miller, Lud Wray and Lou Little, of Penn . . . Little Bill Johnston within point, game, set and world's tennis championship at the Manheim Cricket Club—and Big Bill Tilden then knocking him over . . . Among the spectators: Theda Bara.

Another Philadelphian, William S. Houser, told me one time about the three-horse double-deck buses that ran on Broad Street from "the Hump" (Huntingdon Street) to Jackson Street, where the stable was located. The stable later became a fight club and it was there that Bob Fitzsimmons and Joe Grim waged a memorable battle.

All of this, I should add, was before my time in the town—and much of it was even before my time. But I felt the pangs of nostalgia and shed a few quiet tears in my column when they started to tear down the old Earle Theater on Market Street some years ago. Thousands of Philadelphians had seen a host of great performers there through the years, when it was the only big vaudeville or variety house in the town. And the stage shows there were the first ones I reviewed for a newspaper.

And, more than that . . .

Well, it wasn't just another theater they were tearing down—to me—but the symbol of a more carefree day in the land, of a lusty music which swept the country and made idols out of bespectacled guys like Benny Goodman and the late Tommy Dorsey, and of a long-gone generation they called the jitterbug (*circa* 1936 to . . . well, let's say Pearl Harbor).

Back in the thirties (and when you think of them now, in this Era of the H-bomb, you don't remember the heartaches of the Depression), a new music had come along in America and a new language with it, and the boys and girls literally danced in the streets. They danced in the streets in front of the Earle, because Goodman was going to be there—Goodman and Harry James and Gene Krupa and Teddy Wilson and Lionel Hampton. And Goodman was king of this new music, the King of Swing, and these were the talented members of his royal retinue.

So they would line up with the dawn on cold winter mornings to be sure of their seats in the palace of rhythm, and they would be dancing all cares away, the kids with bright cheeks and bright eyes that didn't bother to—or couldn't—stare into a hazy and troubled future. And they were laughing and gay then, like children before they tumble into the adult years, gay with the happy music and the freshness of the morning and the goodness of the days and—perhaps—the future that was theirs.

It had come into being suddenly, this swing—an offspring of Dixieland and the blues and marches from New Orleans, a tot in toddling clothes that stowed away on the Mississippi riverboats and finally wound up in a Greenwich Village spot where a couple of guys named Riley and Farley were playing "The Music Goes 'Round and 'Round." And it went 'round and 'round the land, a snowball of sound, full of mellow notes and exciting runs and driving rhythms. And they worried about the kids who pledged allegiance to and bestowed admiration upon the new music.

The sociologists analyzed and the psychologists pontificated and the editorialists poured worries into print. They wondered if this could be some weird and abnormal flight from the apple on the corner, the beckoning bread line. And they gave the symptoms and symbols fancy names, and they wrote highfalutin phrases around them. Well, a few years later, hundreds and thousands of those jitterbugs they had been wondering and worrying about went off to a lot of strange places like Tarawa and Salerno and Guadalcanal and Saint-Lo. And their girls went into the factories to make them the weapons of war.

And they did right well, those kids who had clapped hands and stomped feet and screamed delight to the beat of swing music, who had made a clarinet man the Pied Piper of Pandemonium. They were still going off to strange places, like Seoul, and leaving their girls behind them, when they began to tear down the Earle. But it was different. It was preordained, inescapable. You reached a certain age and you knew what your life would be, for a while.

Then, back in the thirties, Hitler was still a name you laughed at and Russia was one you didn't think about much at all. And, although there was the Depression, a guy always had a chance. He could take his fling with the fates.

And now, in this day of the H-bomb and a cold war that never ends, with the old Earle made into a scrap pile and quickly replaced by a modern new store, I keep remembering those fine clear mornings and those bright-faced kids. I remember them dancing so gaily in the streets of the town.

They dance today still, of course—if not in the streets. But it isn't the same and nothing's the same, and you will pardon me for grieving a little about an old theater that had long since seen its best days, because it somehow symbolized a time in America when kids, many of whom would die on beaches like Utah and in forests like Hürtgen, could dance in the streets with the zest of living.

Chapter IX

Society's Like the Old Gray Mare

In her day, no doubt, this woman had walked erectly, head high, manner confident, bearing aristocratic. But now she was old and wrinkled and stooped, and able to move only by making use of the two canes she carried. I watched her one afternoon some years ago as she came out of the Bellevue-Stratford Hotel and started across Broad Street at Walnut.

The solicitous traffic policeman hurried toward her and tried to take her by the arm to escort her across the busy intersection. She shook him off roughly.

"When I need help, young man," she snapped, "I'll call your superiors and have you assigned to me permanently."

Then, with painful precision, completely ignoring the heavy traffic around her, she made her own way across the wide street.

That, it seems to me, just about sums up the state of Philadelphia society today. It retains its pride and it carries its head high. But, like the old gray mare, it just ain't what it used to be. Its homes are not so palatial, its parties not so lavish, its finances not so affluent and its influence not so powerful as they once were.

Only members of Philadelphia society are really concerned about members of Philadelphia society today.

Times have changed. The days when shopgirls and five-and-dime store clerks were supposed to read all about the doings of those born into the aristocratic class with wide eyes and futile hopes, wishing they could be part of such a rich and gay life, have gone for good. The inhabitants of the *Social Register*, or *Blue Book*—or Stud Book, as cynical denizens of the newspaper city rooms have called it for years—have lost their gloss and been stripped of their glamour.

Patty, the poor working girl, just doesn't care any more. She and all of her laboring companions from the row houses and shabby streets were handed new idols for their daydreaming when the movies came along and Hollywood became a symbol of the mad whirl, the extravagant parties. And now Patty and friends have not only the movie world but the worlds of the stage, radio, television and popular music to fall back upon for their eager, expectant reading and idle, dreamy thoughts. The descendants of "Palinurus Peeper," a gossip columnist dating back to colonial times, helped to bring that about.

Many other things have changed for society, too. The famous town houses have been gone for years from Rittenhouse Square, which is now the apartment house sector of the midtown, still ritzy but in a more brash, less traditional modern fashion.

In the early part of the century the city's social scene had been dominated by the most fabulous town house of all, the one at 1801 Walnut Street. Mrs. Sarah Drexel Fell Van Rensselaer lived there in splendor, ruled there as the "hostess with the mostest" of her day, and died there in 1929. It was a significant year. It was the year the Great Depression began. And, as the Depression marked the end of an era in America's social life, her death marked the conclusion of an era in Philadelphia's society life.

The Depression played no favorites. It never bothered to even consult the *Social Register*. Numerous fortunes disappeared and town houses were a drug on the market. Mrs. Van Rensselaer's was closed down. It was vacant for ten years and then, in 1942, it became the Penn Athletic Club.

Another era reached a somewhat belated conclusion two years

after that when the huge 130-room mansion, Whitemarsh Hall, where Mrs. Edward T. Stotesbury had lived and reigned over society in the suburbs through the twenties, was sold to the Pennsylvania Salt Manufacturing Company. Mrs. Stotesbury, who had entertained with regal splendor on money that came from the Drexel-Morgan banking house, died two years later in 1933. The mansion on the top of the hill which, along with thirty-eight of the three hundred acres surrounding it, had been bought for a mere bagatelle—the paltry sum of $167,000—became a research center for the salt firm. The other acres of Mrs. Stotesbury's land are now Whitemarsh Village, one of the most pleasant and attractive of the many new surburban housing developments.

And that's the way it has been.

Actually the social scene had moved from the town houses in the city to the country houses on the Main Line long before Mrs. Van Rensselaer's death. The automobile came in, the *Social Register* folks moved out. They had cars to get them from business establishment to beautiful estate in a hurry. But the Depression changed that, too. Large estates became smaller estates and many palatial old homes have been vacated.

A changing way of American life, a changing social scene—in the broad sense—was at work again. The cost of maintaining large estates became prohibitive for many families. Servants were harder to find and even more difficult to keep. There were better wages elsewhere. And although the affairs on the Main Line and in Chestnut Hill (where many of the older families still reside) go on apace, they have become progressively smaller and steadily less ostentations.

With this development there has come a slow but definite fading out of the cult of ancestor worship, which for many years had assumed ridiculous proportions and was, I think, an unhealthy aspect of Philadelphia life. Families which hadn't done anything constructive or worth while or significant for decades carried their snobbish badges of self-importance boldly because their ancestors had been "colonials" (Philadelphia society's birth took place long before the Revolutionary War) or "signers" (of the Declaration of Independence, that is). Because of this, hundreds of persons who contributed nothing to the advancement of the city or civic life felt that they were automatically important by reason of birth and deserved respect and obeisance from the public at large. Some of the members of these old families were, in fact, victims of a new ailment which is called on television "tired blood."

Remnants of this arrogance about family name are still around, but the attitude has diminished steadily in the last couple of decades and some day it may vanish entirely from the town. The Depression and the recent wars and perhaps plain old common sense all helped to do the job. Snobbery is still present in the drawing room from time to time, no doubt, but it is not displayed so glaringly in public. And, as its influence has waned, society has gone more democratic.

Some of my best friends are society people. One of my favorite Philadelphians is Francis R. Strawbridge, Jr., a tall, handsome and thoroughly engaging gentleman. He is an executive with the family store—Strawbridge & Clothier—naturally, but he also does a great deal of worthy work for the blind (and many other welfare and charity organizations) and he is one of the most naturally democratic guys you would want to know.

Now I have said that the influence of the old families in the city's life has waned. But that is not to say that the old families do not have influence. Particularly in the insurance world—and that is a busy and important one in Philadelphia—they retain a solid power. But they play a much smaller role in the industrial and business worlds than they once did.

And it is a fact, too, and an important one, that they have played a smaller part in the redevelopment of Philadelphia—the building and the rebuilding, the improvement of the port and the airport, the modernization programs—than the new and not-so-tired blood which has come to the town from many fresh sources, from many different nationalities, from different religions, from men whose forefathers haven't been here for years and who, in many cases, lifted themselves by their own bootstraps. That our town is finally getting things done impressively after lazily and backwardly ignoring its problems before World War II is not principally or particularly due to the old families at all. The growth, the improvement of the town has been nurtured and carried out largely by the newer names—by men like banker William Fulton Kurtz, chairman of the board of the Pennsylvania Company; financier Albert M. Greenfield, with all of his interests and properties tied up with the city's future; big businessman and former bricklayer John B. Kelly, undoubtedly our leading Horatio Alger story; progressive and liberal former Mayor Clark; progressive and liberal present Mayor Dilworth; Arthur C. Kaufmann, executive head of Gimbels department store; Harry G. Schad, vice president of the Atlantic Refining Co.; philanthropist Lessing J. Rosenwald; realtor Frank G. Binswanger; Geoffrey S. Smith, president of the Girard Trust Corn Exchange Bank; H. A. Batten, board chairman of N. W. Ayer & Son; F. Carter Schaub, general manager of Sears, Roebuck & Co.; a number of Pennsylvania Railroad officials headed by president James M. Symes; and no doubt many others I am unintentionally neglecting.

To these names should be added those of persons like Mrs. John Frederick Lewis, a member of the Board of Education and a patron of the arts; and Judge Edwin O. Lewis, whose particular interest for years has been the Independence Mall projects.

The list of persons who could be called upon for leadership in programs, projects and causes—and have been again and again—could go on and on. And it would be unfair to strike out society names in one fell swoop, and that is not my intention at all. Biddle. Morris. Cadwalader (the ones with the single "l" are the more stylish ones). Ingersoll. Bullitt. Hopkinson. These and many others are familiar and worthy ones in many facets of the city's life, leaders almost always in the cultural programs. Charles Meigs Biddle Cadwalader devoted a quarter of a century to "his" Academy of Natural Sciences until he retired in 1951. The Zoological Society was the pet of his brother, Dr. Williams Biddle Cadwalader, who had been its president from 1926 until his death in June, 1957.

The newspaper families play highly important roles, too, in the city's life, not only through the contributions made by their organs of public opinion but in personal activities.

The three newspapers wage a constant editorial campaign for needed improvements, for necessary changes. They help to bring a host of projects to completion. They urge and they recommend and they admonish and they warn—and they serve as excellent watchdogs against both municipal corruption and civic lethargy.

The McLeans (Robert McLean is president and publisher) are a retiring family which remains in the background while "Nearly Everybody Reads the *Bulletin*" they publish—a slogan that has gained national prominence and is as familiar to *New Yorker* readers as Peter Arno's cartoons. The *Bulletin's* new building opposite the Thirtieth Street Station is the most modern newspaper plant in the country.

Making a laudable fetish of accuracy, complete in its coverage, brightly written and edited by a staff of many skills and talents, level-headed in tone and rarely angry or excited in its editorials, the *Bulletin* has earned the right to its slogan. It is not only the largest evening newspaper in America but its Sunday paper, climbing steadily, has already gone over the three-quarter-of-a-million mark in circulation, although it has only been published since the demise of the *Record*.

As the *Bulletin* reflects the McLeans, so the *Inquirer* reflects its young publisher, Walter H. Annenberg. He is continuously active in civic and social affairs and likes to take a personal hand in issues which have stimulated his interest or resentment. His newspaper is aggressive, hard-hitting in its crusades and campaigns, of which there are many.

Since he inherited this morning newspaper from his colorful father, M. L. Annenberg, the never restful son has built a publishing empire for himself, *TV Guide* and *Seventeen* magazine particularly having proved to be remarkable successes. The *Inquirer's* Sunday circulation is well over a million, which would indicate that Philadelphians do a heap of Sunday newspaper reading.

New life has been breathed into the third of the town's newspapers, the tabloid *Daily News*, since it was bought several years ago by big builder and political power Matthew H. McCloskey. McCloskey, who is treasurer of the Democratic National Committee, turned the newspaper into a Democratic party organ after years in which it had been a straight, unveering Republican mouthpiece.

Both the *Bulletin* and *Inquirer* are avowedly independent but usually Republican, the latter in a much more outspoken fashion. The *Daily News* is now published by David Stern, author of *Francis*, the novel about the talking mule, and son of the former publisher of the *Record*. He took over early in 1957. Emphasizing features and brevity, it is snappily edited and has gained considerably more respect from the public. It once had hardly any at all. McCloskey, who poured large bundles of cash into improving both paper and plant, is now chairman of the board.

And so many new names have come along to join those old ones which go back to a more staid and probably more stuffy Philadelphia. Society has changed. Aloof barriers have slowly gone down. Snobbish attitudes have quietly diminished. Society, like all of us, is living in the second half of the twentieth century right now, and almost all of its members finally realize it. Moreover, and more importantly, most of them are satisfied and happy with their more democratic and more American way of life.

Let me tell you a couple of little stories.

In 1957 the Devon Horse Show and Country Fair Committee —this week-long event is one of the highlights of the year on the Main Line each summer—presented none other than Louis (Satchmo) Armstrong in its annual benefit concert for the Bryn Mawr Hospital. Now Satchmo is on my own list of the Ten Greatest Americans of Our Day, but he isn't on any list of guests for any party at the Barclay. The good ladies took him right in stride.

At a committee meeting to discuss arrangements for the concert, one sedate lady asked what compositions Mr. Armstrong would play.

"Tin Roof Blues, When the Saints Go Marching In, Blueberry Hill . . ." she was told.

For a few seconds a shocked expression wreathed her face. But she recovered quickly. She smiled. The meeting went on. The concert was a happy success.

Story number two:

A delightful old woman, a great-grandmother in one of the better-known families, has been served for many years by the jewelry firm of S. Kind & Sons. (The favorite firm with top society, of course, is J. E. Caldwell & Co., with Bailey, Banks & Biddle in the runner-up spot.)

The conversations of Philip Kind, Jr., with this woman, mostly by phone, had been limited largely to wedding present orders and words of praise for President Eisenhower.

He was slightly amazed therefore when she phoned the day after the heavyweight championship bout between ancient Archie Moore and young Floyd Patterson, told him enthusiastically what a great fight it had been, and ordered a set of silver for the newly born baby of the newly crowned titleholder.

Even those exclusive assembly balls have felt the impact of the measured tread of time and the shifting temper of the times. The invitations are limited still, loosely, to the descendants of the original members. But money, marriages and modern mores have wrought inevitable changes.

Actually the breakdown began about half a century ago, it was pointed out by former *Record* political reporter Thomas P. O'Neil, now public relations man for the Pennsylvania Manufacturers Association, in the chapter ("Where Patience Is a Vice") he wrote on Philadelphia for Robert S. Allen's book, *Our Fair City.*

At that time, O'Neil explained, Edward T. Stotesbury "threatened to take his millions away from Philadelphia if his two daughters were not invited to the traditional function. They were." But the Cadwaladers stayed home.

Several years later the son and daughter of multimillionaire Joseph E. Widener were also admitted.

Once upon a time the slightest breath of scandal would rule out an invitation. Divorce simply barred one. But divorces have become as common as martinis in the social set—well, almost—and the rules are not so firmly applied as they were.

The male is the dominant figure in the assemblies. If a man marries a woman who is not from one of the old families, she rates an invitation. But if a woman of an old family marries a man who isn't, she has a tough job ahead to crash him into the ball.

A male can get a divorce and continue to be invited, I understand. But if the wife has landed the divorce, she isn't invited.

And, like the old gray mare and society in general, the assembly balls ain't what they used to be. They hardly retain the magic lure they once held. They do not prompt the awesome esteem of half a century ago. Some of the luster has been worn off through the years and years and years of their being and by the more cynical world of today.

As one member of the Assembly—and one of the town's leading citizens—told me early this year:

"I pay my dues, but I haven't gone for years. It's so stuffy you find yourself dancing with your wife all night."

He didn't mean it in complete seriousness. But the casual remark held the kernel of truth.

Chapter X

Each Day Tells of Many Lives

The day begins in our town when the trucks unload their cargoes and it ends when the taprooms unload their customers. Between those first noises that come with the darkness slipping into dawn and those last voices saying good night on sleeping streets, between raucous teeming Dock Street on the east and the bustling Sixty-ninth Street section on the west, between the hustling sprawling Navy Yard on the south and the big-lawned, eye-filling houses of Chestnut Hill on the north, you meet a day's quota of people, acquire a new batch of impressions, hear some old truths spoken, and are pleasantly surprised by the fact that scenes never lose their interest.

Every day's a long day, but nobody seems to get quite enough of them. And each day tells of many lives. You get a haircut and learn that your barber, Tony Turtzo, out on Sixtieth Street, still uses the old expression "heavy date," which you thought had gone out with hip flasks, flappers and rumble seats. It sounds good. It sounds like youth.

You step into a cab owned by John McDonald and see on the sun visor a crucifix, a St. Theresa medal, a Jewish scroll and Star of David, because the day driver is Frank Baragilo and the night driver is Arthur Heissen. And that looks good. It looks the way the world wants it to be.

You stroll into Rittenhouse Square and find that it looks like a combination nursery school and kindergarten. The midtown mothers congregate there with their young ones for health from the sun and the silent sky, and conversation from wagging tongues. The mothers try to outdo each other in bragging about their offspring or social position. But a few days ago, you learn, one mother went too far. She wheeled her child into the square in a new, mink-lined carriage. The others cannot hope to keep up this trend. They are cutting her dead.

You get a shine from Daddy and then you walk along Broad Street and three little boys bid for the job.

"Just got a shine," you tell them.

"That's a *shine?*" shouts one of them, grinning from ear to ear. And you hope he grows up to be a rich and famous comedian.

You ride a trolley on Market Street. A woman passenger steps off. As the trolley begins to move away, a boy notices she has left a package on the seat. He shouts to the motorman to hold the door, races after the woman. The conductor doesn't hear him. The light changes. The trolley moves off. The boy catches up to the woman, but the trolley has gone. All he can do now is wait for another one. Cost of a good deed: an extra fare.

You see two young blind men standing outside the entrance to the Overbrook School for the Blind, waiting for a bus to come along. They are students there, and they wear dark glasses and carry canes. As the bus arrives, one of them starts to feel his way through the open door toward a seat, the bus driver getting up to help him.

The other young man, who had come to the corner to see his friend off, stands by the bus door as the friend enters. Then, standing on the corner, he listens intently for the bus door to close, the signal that his friend is safely inside and will soon be on his way. Finally the bus door closes. The young man looks in the general direction of the bus, raises his cane in a farewell and shouts, quite naturally: "See you soon!" Then he turns and taps his way back into the world of the blind.

You get that call from the woman who has gotten loaded in a bar at two o'clock in the afternoon. Either this woman makes a lot of calls—or there are a lot of these women. The calls are periodic.

"I'll give you a real story," the woman says in a husky voice, phrases falling from her tongue with liquid difficulties, her words slurred.

"Yes, what is it?" you ask, knowing very well what it is. It is about her husband. He is a beast.

"We don't use family squabbles in the column," you explain.

"Family squabble?" she exclaims, her voice high-pitched, her tone one of utter amazement. "This is a big story."

"I'm sorry, but it sounds like a family squabble to me."

"Well now I'll tell you, this is a story, one you can dig into. And I'll tell you, you'll find plenty of dirt, too, when you start digging."

"But it's still a family affair."

"Now I'll tell you, this is a lot more than that. This is a story. It's a lot more than a family squabble."

"Well, why is it?"

"Why? Why? Because everybody should know about *this* man. He's a disgrace to the whole city, that's what he is."

And come evening time, walking along Walnut Street, you meet comic Harry (Lifty) Lewis, home from Garden State Track.

"I had the best day at the track I've ever had in my life," says Lifty.

"Yeah?"

"Yeah, I got a ride home."

Always the comic.

I remember the day that Al Schmid, one of the boys from the streets of Philadelphia who figured things in this country were nice enough to fight for, came home from the jungles of the Pacific. Private First Class Albert A. Schmid, of 7454 Rockwell Avenue, if you please. One of the biggest heroes of World War II.

Private Schmid of the U.S. Marine Corps killed two hundred Japs on Guadalcanal with his blazing machine gun. And then he spent a lot of weeks in the Naval Hospital at San Diego, California. And when he came home, he didn't come marching. And there were no bands playing, and nobody made any speeches, and some of the things Al liked about this country—a frozen lake for ice skating, a swimming pool, a funny movie, his girl's smile—he could not see because he was blind.

It had been a triumphant journey across the continent from San Diego. Crowds gathered at every stop and there were eagerly presented gifts for him and there was the excited talk. "He's that kid who killed two hundred Japs. Schmid. Gee, he's nice-looking. Yeah, that's the boy that knocked off two hundred of them. . . ."

"But he didn't seem to care anything about the crowds or the presents," Robert Hudson, a Texan and a pharmacist's mate who had accompanied him on the journey, told me when Al's train pulled into the North Philadelphia Station.

"He just wanted to get home."

I remember a truck driver named Eddie, who was a victim of unusual injustice in our town. It was as Eddie the truck driver said. It was a trap. Anyway you looked at it, it was a trap.

"I drives a truck over the road," Eddie said. "For years I drove from New York to Maine. For a few months now I have been goin' to Philly. That is how I got to read your column.

"I have a gripe about your city, and I want to tell you about it. A few days ago I was arolling for New York and was headin' for Roosevelt Boulevard. A cop drives up and pulls me over and tells me I just passed a sign saying NO TRUCKS.

"I argued that he was wrong but I gets the ticket. After he leaves, I had to walk back to see for myself where he said the sign was. No sign, so I says to a fellow standing on the curb, 'Do you see a sign that says no trucks?'

"He says no. I see a mailman and I ask him, and he says, 'Yes, no trucks allowed on Castor Avenue,' and he shows me the sign. And guess what it said. I got it right here. I wrote it down.

"Here's what it says: COMMERCIAL VEHICLES EXCLUDED.

"Boy, is that a trap! I know I'm not real smart, but I am not real dumb either. But when they puts signs like that up for us truck drivers, it isn't very fair.

"That must be the ritziest street in your town. COMMERCIAL VEHICLES EXCLUDED. Man, is that fancy! No wonder no trucks is allowed."

And there was Barney. Barney, the former Mayor.

His full name was Bernard Samuel, but everybody called him Barney. He was a little fellow with a full, round face. And he was, to be sure, a political hack, a man who was moved up through the ranks by the powerful GOP machine that had always exercised tremendous influence in his own South Philadelphia bailiwick.

He wasn't learned and he wasn't well educated—except in the political school of hard knocks and playing ball—and he wasn't eloquent. I remember him getting up at one of the early civil defense meetings during World War II and telling those assembled that the town would have to get some more sire-eens.

But he was a goodhearted little man, anxious to please everybody, and he had acquired a host of friends by the time he died. You didn't have to admire Barney, but you couldn't help liking him. You could blast Barney for something in a column and if you happened to run into him that evening, he would slap you on the shoulder and say, "Pretty rough on me today." And then you would both laugh about it and you were still friends because, to Barney—as he had been trained through the years—politics was something of a game, too. And you took the bad with the good and were a sport about it.

The present leaders, I suppose, are more honest, more progressive. But they also are afflicted with something of a god complex, the feeling that they can do no wrong, that they know everything and nobody else knows much of anything. They quiver angrily at the slightest public criticism of their actions or their programs, and they bleed words of protest by the thousands.

Barney wouldn't have bothered. Life is short. Politics *is* to a considerable extent a game. Perhaps there is something to be said for both sides, both ways.

In addition to being short, life, for the most part, is the state of being between a smile and a tear. And it can change focus quickly. I remember a strange little drama that was played out several years ago on a busy, crowded, typical street in Philadelphia.

The street is Sixth Street. There was a home in the 1300 block there where life had been moving along in its casual way—between heart throb and heartbreak. Then a man was killed in a holdup by a teen-age gang known as the Green Street Counts. One of the boys in the gang was Socrates R. Cantoral, who lived in that home.

Only three squares away, at 962 North Sixth Street, there was a home that had been haunted for two years by fear. And as sadness took over the one home, where a family awaited with dread the verdict of a court on the future of a son, joy returned to the other, when it received the official information from Uncle Sam that a son was coming home. Private First Class John M. Jankovits, the son, was one of the first American prisoners to be released by the Reds in Korea. He was coming home. The anxiety was ended.

For the one boy, who had mistreated freedom, it was now denied. For the other, who had fought for freedom, it was now regained. And the two homes, only a few squares away from each other, in those weeks, could have been a million miles apart.

There was a bum who left a story behind, too. When you're a bum you have a slightly different slant on the world. A loaf of bread becomes a cake. A warm spot becomes a comfortable living room.

Now the benches in the old Broad Street Station, which disappeared from the midtown scene some years ago and was replaced by Penn Center buildings, were hard. They didn't provide the comfort of a bed with a big, soft mattress, but at least it was warm in the station. You were inside and it wasn't a bad place at all for a guy who was down on his luck to spend the night. For a bum, it was like lying down in the lap of luxury.

That was the backdrop for the strange story of a guy who used two tickets to Miami for sleeping purposes only. The story began when relatives of steel executive William H. Donner, of Villanova, purchased tickets to Miami with Pullman reservations. Somehow the tickets were lost. Pullman arrangements were canceled, of course, but there was nothing that could be done about the tickets.

For Donner's relatives, it was money lost. For the bum, it was sanctuary found. He lived high and mighty for weeks. Each night he reclined on a warm bed—a bench in the station. The tickets made it possible. He didn't use them. He made no attempt to sell them, so no charge could ever be lodged against him. All he did was show them.

They would come around in the nights and nudge him or shake him and get ready to kick him out because the station was no hotel and all-night sleeping was not allowed there. And then the bum would rise majestically and show them that he was no bum. Slowly, as though he had been insulted and resented the intrusion upon his private life, this ridiculous questioning of his financial status, he would take the tickets from his pocket.

Why, this man was going to Miami. Just passing an hour or so here. . . . And so to sleep again, in luxury.

In time, of course, the happy nights had to come to an end. It was inevitable. The tickets were displayed too often. Suspicions grew and finally one night the Pennsylvania Railroad police picked up the guy with the tickets to Miami and ended his long date with luxury. And again he had to start riding the rods to somewhere, hunting for some small warm corner of the world.

Chapter XI

When Evening Arrives in the Town

PHILADELPHIA is not a city for night life. It is not a night club city, but that is no reflection on the night clubs it has. It is not particularly noted for its dining places, and that is out-and-out libel on its restaurants. It is not especially known for its hotels, and that is unfair to some of the hotels it has.

There are a number of reasons for the situation. First, Philadelphia *is* a City of Homes, and the people generally like to stay in them. They have been staying in them more than ever, incidentally, since television became the national recreation and turned living rooms into theaters. Additionally, with the exodus of thousands of families in recent years to suburban houses and places with a little ground around them to work, the home has become both more demanding—if more pleasant—and the task of "going into town" has become less intriguing.

The neighborhood taproom has always been a favorite gathering spot, too. No taxes are added to the bill in McMahon's saloon. And there Joe Doakes, frequently cowed by a headwaiter and fearful of how much to tip who in a fancy club, can become a big shot—fleetingly, at least—simply by ordering a round of beer for the boys.

Secondly, Philadelphia is *not* a transient city. It has its share of conventions, to be sure, and it gets its quota of visiting families. But it doesn't get the massive number of conventions that a New York or Chicago, principal cities for an entire region, will handle. The Quaker City, remember, is only some ninety miles from New York. Inevitably it must sit in the shadow cast by Gotham.

Nor does the town ordinarily get the free-spending, hefty expense account buying-and-selling sessions that these cities consistently entertain. As a result, the restaurants and the night clubs, for the most part, and the hotels to a lesser extent, must depend on the same clientele week after week—and there just aren't enough of these people to go around.

And, to make it even tougher for the places selling drinks—and the night clubs especially—there is a state law which forces them to close on Sundays, which means the midnight hour on Saturday nights. This costs them dearly on what otherwise would be their best night and likely could be their best day. An ironic aspect of all this is that the business goes to the scores of private clubs—many of them joints, some of them downright disreputable—which dot every neighborhood of the city.

These spots reap the benefit from all of the people who are having a big week end on the town, liquor included, or are in the mood to keep going on a Saturday night fling, although they pay less for their various licenses and have much less overhead. Theoretically—by law, that is—these places are supposed to be organizational, the original charters for them dating back many years, but actually most of them are "one-man clubs," the owners being concerned only with profits over the bar and faking the books they are required to keep.

Early in 1957 Mayor Dilworth, acting on his own, and unexpectedly, announced that he was relaxing enforcement of the state's blue laws to give the people more places to go and to lure more conventions into town. His action paved the way for more Sunday sports events—for years only baseball and football had been permitted—and set the stage for the town's first Sunday musical concerts and shows of all kinds.

But liquor sales are still barred.

The net result of this old and general situation, along with the steadily increasing cost of living and the growth of country clubs in the growing suburbs as additional factors, has been this:

A city which had some twenty clubs playing entertainment world headliners, or well-known performers at least, in the lush days right after World War II, now has a mere handful. It has, in fact, only two midtown spots operating with regular floor shows, and both of these are closed through most of the summer.

Some twenty clubs or musical bars—a raft of these sprung up during the war—have fallen by the wayside in the last five or six years, including Frankie Palumbo's Click, with its biggest bar in the world, and the Embassy, operated by Sam Silber and Herb Smiler, which had done well even during the Depression, when it was a favorite society spot. Click had played the biggest names available. The Embassy had also been one of the town's finest dining places.

The two night clubs operating in the midtown now are the Latin Casino, which is on a par with the best in the nation—the Copacabana and Latin Quarter in New York, the Chez Paree in Chicago—and the Celebrity Room, a smaller, more intimate room which plays top names most of the time, although its shows are not nearly so expensive as those bought by the larger place.

The Celebrity Room features, of all things, a lighted replica of Rodin's "The Kiss" in a corner of its dining room facing the stage and thereby hands its comics a batch of new gags. The club is owned by the Lerner family, papa Sam, handsome older son Mac and young son Stanley, who has ambitions to be a comedian himself. Two insurance men were previous owners of this spot, which points up a fact: The days when racketeers controlled clubs are long gone in this town. Some racket guys are still involved in small operations but none are connected with the big places.

The Latin Casino, for instance, is owned and operated by Dave Dushoff and Dallas Gerson, who are also partners in a profitable tile business. The club, a tastefully decorated room seating more than six hundred persons and the flagship of the town's night life, is their hobby. They like to make money out of it, of course, but it is still a hobby. They enjoy the atmosphere. They like to be hosts. They like being a part of show business, even though theirs is the back-door entrance to the field. And presenting all of the big names—Harry Belafonte, Joe E. Lewis, Sammy Davis, Jr., Lena Horne, *et al.*—they are fortunate that they have the more steady and predictable tile business. One night of heavy rain or snow when they have one of their big budget shows can completely kill their chances of avoiding any loss for the week. So they are also fortunate that they have a sense of humor.

They make a good pair. In 1957, when the club was closed down, they took off on a motor trip to the West Coast. They were cutting across the upper part of Texas when Dallas suggested that they spend a day in Dallas, Texas.

"But that's three hundred miles out of our way," Dave complained.

"Pahdner," said Dallas, "if there was a town named Dushoff, and we were six hundred miles out of the way, you'd still want to go."

They went to Dallas.

Aside from the two midtown clubs with floor shows and all of the musical bars, many featuring girlie shows, there are a number of other spots well known in the town.

Both Chubby's, just across the Delaware in Jersey, and Sciolla's, in the northeast section, are big places presenting the top record stars. Harry Carroll has had his little spot in West Philly for many years. Florence O'Boyle's Cadillac Sho-Bar has been in operation for a long time. Then there are the "music rooms," the Blue Note, Pep's, the Showboat and the Red Hill Inn (also in Jersey), which offer the leading jazz attractions.

And, most of all, there is Palumbo's, which certainly must be a modern landmark. If Philadelphia is the City of Homes, this spot can just as accurately be called the Club of Banquets. And it has that familiar Philadelphia motif, one which recurs again and again in every phase of the town's life. Palumbo's is old, it has stayed in the same place—a thickly populated section of South Philly—and it's always been in the family. In 1860 an Italian immigrant named Anthony Palumbo opened a restaurant at Ninth Street near Catharine. In 1884 the restaurant became a club at

824 Catharine Street. It's still there, it's still being operated by the Palumbos, with Frankie at the main controls.

This big club, in a section of squat row houses, has been the scene through the years of thousands of wedding parties, birthday parties, wedding anniversary parties, fraternal parties, bowling league banquets, baseball league banquets, retirement parties, testimonial dinners, going-away-to-war parties, home-from-war parties. And very few residents, very few of Philadelphia's millions, haven't been there at one time or another.

Many families have written their history there, through the generations. First, the wedding announcement party, the shower from the girls. Then the marriage party. And later on all of the anniversary affairs. Then a daughter and the beginning of the same routine for her.

Adjoining Palumbo's is the CR Club, one of the classier private clubs serving excellent food and providing entertainment. Another is the RDA Club, which isn't too far from City Hall. Don Battles is a gracious host at this club. Other well-known private clubs with reputations for good food are the Vesper, MLA, and 2-4.

Speaking of hosts, Philadelphia has a goodly number of those elegant artists from a calling that unfortunately is becoming lost—the maître d'hôtel or headwaiter, men with style in service and talent where food is concerned. Few are willing now, in these days, to go through the years of preparation, and those remaining on the scene point up the future loss.

You will find topflight men at all of the leading hotels—the brand-new, 1,000-room Sheraton in the new Penn Center, first to be built in the midtown in more than three decades; the Warwick, certainly one of the best-run hotels in the country; the well-known Bellevue-Stratford, the Benjamin Franklin, the Barclay on Rittenhouse Square, the John Bartram, the Drake. . . . Incidentally, the Warwick, where all of the visiting baseball teams stay, is at an edge of the city as it was originally laid out by William Penn. And it's only at Seventeenth Street. Penn's "green countrie towne" has grown a bit.

In addition to the hotel experts, there are a number of other knowing gentlemen at work here and there about the area. There is José Marva, the talented man with a salad at Orsatti's Pump

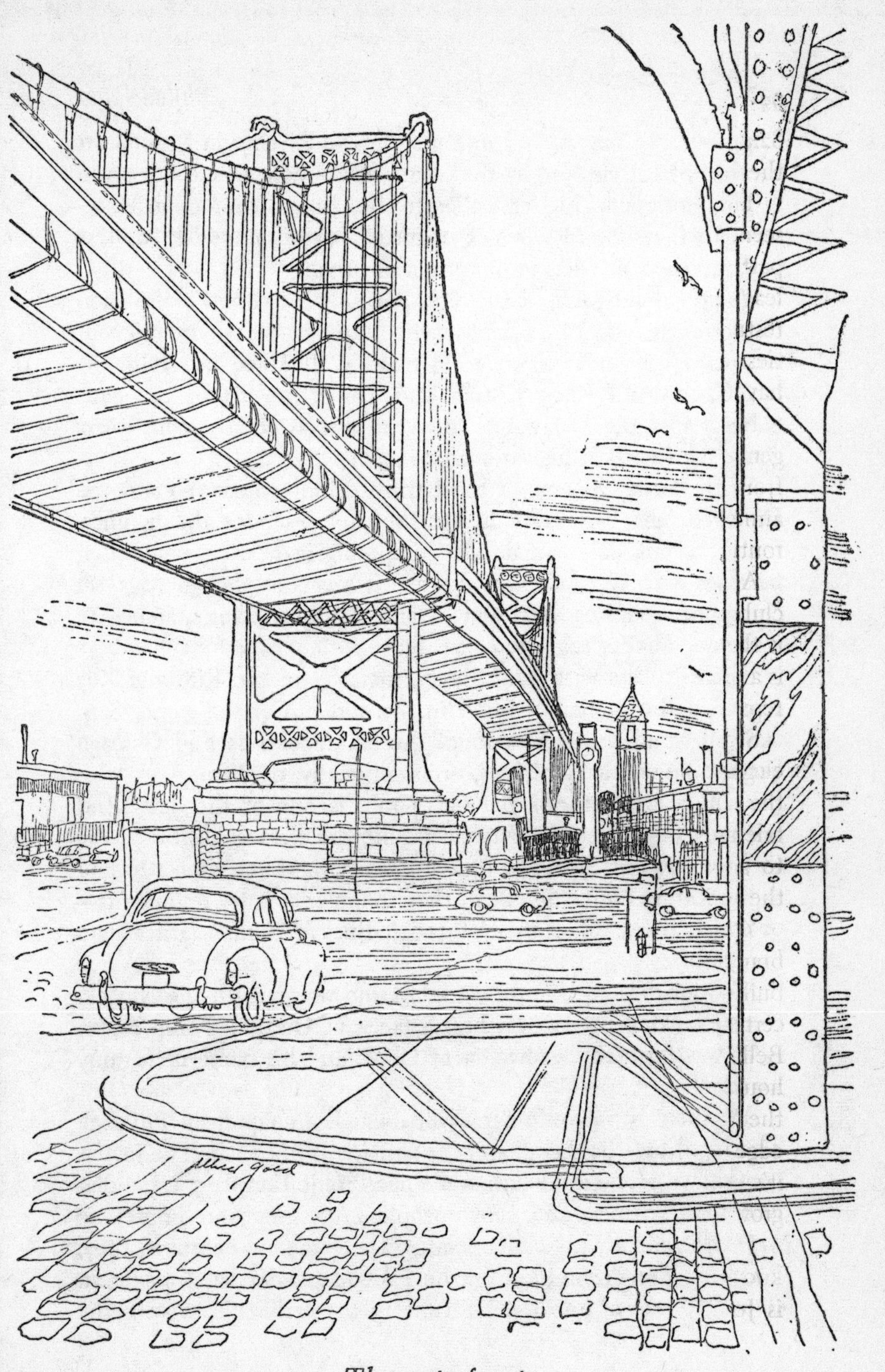

The waterfront

Room. Marva has worked in Paris, on the Riviera, in Vienna, in Cairo, in Brussels, and at the Savoy in London, where he served his apprenticeship. He was called to the Hotel Shamrock in Houston as wine steward when it opened, became homesick for this city, returned, and has no intention of leaving.

There is Paul King, of the Sans Souci, an extremely skilled performer with food of all kinds, who learned at the Traymore in Atlantic City. And the veteran Herman Toll, skilled and stylish, at the Capri. And Rudy Kistner and Phil Cappella, of the Sans Souci across the Delaware, who were associated for many years with Jack Lynch at his various local spots.

With Barney Sloane, of the Latin Casino (where veterans Joe DiAngelo and Tony Turchi are the captains), it's the manner. Barney is tall, dark-haired, erect, imposing in bearing. And when he leads a party to a ringside table, it seems as though flags are being unfurled, bands are playing and royalty is being marched to a throne. That's talent, too.

There is class with Sam Singer, manager of the Kite and Key Room in the Benjamin Franklin. An old pro at the game, Sam can tell wonderful stories about the Al Capone days in Chicago because he was in them and, unintentionally, of them.

Frank Cardellino, of the CR Club, is one of the best. And certainly the prettiest is Margie Pirolli, the seating hostess at the Celebrity Room. She's the pleasant kind of girl you expect to find as the seating hostess in one of those popular country restaurants—of which there are so many through Bucks County—rather than in a club.

Mention has to be made, too, of the waiter with the Mother Goosiest name I have ever heard. He is at Orsatti's Pump Room now, was formerly headwaiter at Click, and his name is Tommy Twaddel.

But there is only one name with which a chapter on Philadelphia night life could end, and the name is Jack Lynch. The town's best-known after-dark figure ever since Prohibition days, a familiar face to sportsmen and show people everywhere, an impresario with style, and a suave club operator, Lynch died in February, 1957.

During the Prohibition era he had operated several suburban clubs. He moved into the big time in the early thirties with the opening of the Club Marguery at the Hotel Adelphia. In subsequent years he operated the Walton Roof, the Latin Casino, the Zodiac Room, the Cambridge Club (a private one), the Gold Key Club in New York and, finally, Jack Lynch's Living Room in the Tabu Supper Club.

In a way, his day had passed him by. The big-spending racketeers had gone from the scene. The big money wasn't around. The law was stricter. And the colorful Jack Lynch, born over a neighborhood cafe and christened Dominick Lynch, had always had troubles with the law. He was always, it seemed, being arrested for liquor violations or gambling. Gambling was even more of his life than hosting. He couldn't resist making a wager on anything.

A few days after his death Jerry Gaghan, the gossip columnist for the *Daily News*, wrote of an incident which typified Lynch. The big and always immaculate guy was standing in the lobby of the Hotel Rio (where the Tabu was located) on the night he suffered the stroke which ultimately led to his death. When Lynch was stricken, Gaghan reported, "two of the boys jumped up to support him. Eddie Serody, owner of the Hickory House, was in the phone booth and rushed out to help.

"Dazed and half-blinded by the stroke, Lynch saw Serody coming from the phone booth and thought he might have been calling for a basketball result."

So, naturally, there could have been only one question in Lynch's mind.

"Who win the ball game, Eddie?" he asked. Then he fell into a chair.

Chapter XII

Do You Wish to Order Now?

THE tasty, if sticky, cinnamon bun originated in Philadelphia. So did ice cream. So did pepper pot soup. So did scrapple. You don't have to order them. The town has steaks, too. And sea food and Italian dishes.

It has scores of fine Italian restaurants. There are out-of-the-world specialties at places like Orsatti's Pump Room in the mid-town, the CR Club, and other less fancy places like Ralph's down on South Ninth Street. It's an old Philly custom and Ralph DiSpigno has been operating that restaurant for forty-three years, having inherited it from his father. The chef, John Teti, has been there for sixteen years.

The town has some good German restaurants, best known of which is probably the old Hoffman House. It has many highly rated sea-food houses, like the two Bookbinders' stopping points and Kelly's on Mole Street. But, alas, and strangely, it does not have a single French restaurant.

It does, however, have many excellent restaurants of all kinds—except French. The most nationally famous of all of them, undoubtedly, is Old Original Bookbinders, which dates back to

1863, is on Walnut Street just off Dock down by the water front, has the proper and picturesque *décor* and atmosphere for its location, and is the place all visitors seem to ask about when they want to sample some sea food. It is operated by John Taxin.

Cabdrivers will tell you that it's standard procedure for any conventioneer to hop in and say, "Take me to Bookbinders," on his first or second night in town. Lobsters are taken right from the tanks for serving here. And, incidentally, it has the only manager who lives right on the premises—and a feminine one, as well, in Edna Foster, general manager Joseph Donnolo's assistant. Her apartment is right above the banquet rooms.

There is another well-known Bookbinders on South Fifteenth Street, right in the business district. It's operated by members of the original family (Sam Bookbinder is the boss man) but is a separate enterprise, and the competition between the two is a vigorous one. Sea food is the specialty here, too, with Booky's baked crab a feature.

Popular with the Main Line gentry and midtown businessmen is Helen Sigel's at 1523 Walnut Street. It's operated by Mrs. Helen Sigel Wilson, the well-known golfer and a woman with a delightfully warm personality.

The Capri at 1523 (that's a good number in town) Locust Street is one of the town's smartest intimate supper clubs. It features small shows, boasts an elegant dining room, and serves dinners in style, everything from spaghetti and Chinese food to roast pheasant. An unusual aspect of the town's culinary life is that many of the smarter places make a specialty of Chinese food, even a night club like the Latin Casino. And the very best in that line can be obtained at the leading Chinatown restaurants, one of which is operated by the unofficial mayor of Chinatown, Leong Hop.

High standards are set by the Sans Souci, just a few doors from the Capri. Special attention is devoted to every dish here and the salads are a delight.

Most popular with the sports crowds for years has been Lew Tendler's on South Broad Street. Extremely popular with before-theater crowds and families is the Saxony, where there is a wide variety of dishes, all of them ably prepared. This place is operated by Joe and Ben Stave and Jack Kress, three graduates of the old Embassy.

Sherry's, the newest large restaurant in the town, has the oldest motif, its *décor* being that of the Gay Nineties, and the atmosphere has been reproduced with remarkable fidelity. Shoyer's, way down on Arch Street, dates back to 1874 and features its pot roast and potato pancakes. Mitchell's on Juniper Street maintains top standards and is a steady favorite. It is another happy family operation.

The Stouffer's restaurants have always been popular. There is a branch of the New York Longchamps on Rittenhouse Square.

Excellent food served stylishly can be found at the Sans Souci and the Cherry Hill Inn just across the river, and there are numerous other spots dotting the highways to the shore points which are worth while.

With the movement to the suburbs, there are also many more fine dining places just out of town, like the friendly and delightful Cynwyd Lounge (operated by three popular brothers, Johnny, Tommy and Mundy DeSimone), the new Black Angus, the General Wayne and many others.

The nearest thing to a Greenwich Village spot in the town is very probably Maurice's, which is located on Quince Street, one of the many ancient alleys in the midtown. The structure itself was originally a group of three houses which are more than 250 years old. It was founded by the late Maurice Rotenberg, who was born in Lodz, Poland, and had one love all of his life—music. Classical music.

In the picturesque small dining rooms of this restaurant are stacked thousands and thousands of records—more than 75,000 of them, valued at more than that figure. The music from these is piped into all of the rooms, the speakers being concealed. There is a very special Beethoven Room, which was dear to Maurice's heart, sandwiches are named for composers and conductors, and no matter when you go there, the place "shall be filled with music."

Popular with the classical musicians and visiting actors and actresses is the Russian Inn, which was thirty-five years old in 1957.

And that old local custom again: Sue and Harry Stolwein, the original owners, are still at the helm.

But the most popular place of all with the visiting show people is Frankie Bradley's, and this short, stocky, former boxer, who believes in serving his food highly spiced and in large portions, would be a nationally known column figure if he were operating in New York. His pugilistic career was of brief duration. He was a far cry from his restaurant compatriot, Lew Tendler, in the ring. But he's done mighty well in the food department.

Actors coming into town in plays, headliners playing the clubs, make his spot their hangout during their stay. Many nights you will see the same familiar magazine and newspaper faces there for both dinner and late supper after the show. And Frankie, a fellow who places a high premium on good company and much talk, frequently closes his doors at the proper 2 A.M. hour, locks up, and then turns everything into a private little party of his own. He serves the drinks from behind his tiny bar and he'll stay around as long as the actors will. They usually stay until about dawn, whether they are known night owls like club comic Jackie Miles or simply ordinary mortals caught up by Frankie's good fellowship.

Frankie becomes progressively more philosophical about life and the fates as time passes. Preaching from his bar pulpit, he speaks with increasing intensity as his words and thoughts sound better and better to him. They do not always sound that way to his listeners, but they are never less than interesting.

There is one story that Frankie has recalled many times . . .

One wintry day in 1929, a dozen members of the cast of the Shubert musical, *A Night in Paris*, which was playing in town, walked into Frankie's and sat down in a large corner booth. They looked over the menus and finally decided to order the filet mignon sandwich which was being featured then for a dollar. (Ah, those good old days!) The order was served and a few minutes later a waitress came into the kitchen and told Frankie that one of the men in the large party wanted to see him.

When Frankie reached the booth, a handsome young man with a cleft in his chin stood up and said, "My name is Archie Leach, and just because we're from out of town and we're strangers to you, this is no way to treat us."

He said it bitingly and he pointed to his steak sandwich and to that of the man sitting next to him. "The other ten steaks are wonderful," he said. "Our two are not. What are you going to do about it?"

Frankie looked at the steaks and saw that they were the ends of the filet which the chef had flattened down to use—and which weren't as good as the others. He apologized, and said he would send out two replacements. "And you might as well work on those sandwiches until I get them ready," he added.

The complainant and his companion did nobly by both the originals and the substitutes, and that was the beginning of an unusual friendship between Frankie and Archie Leach.

Archie was a really handsome young fellow then and the girls in the show waged a kind of steady intramural war for his smiles and attentions. He came in almost every night during the long run and the girls would be swooning around him constantly. But he was usually busy ignoring them to swap tales with Frankie. He told Frankie of his boxing days at the age of seventeen. He had fought twice and won. Then in his third fight he was knocked into dreamland—and he quit. Frequently Archie would walk the girls around to the Sylvania Hotel and return to the restaurant to talk until dawn, about any subject under the moon.

They liked each other's company, these two. And every time Archie came to town in another show, he spent the offstage hours with his pal. It was this way until one snowy night in December of 1931. That night, very late, when there wasn't a customer in the restaurant, Archie walked in with a friend, shook off the snow, took off his gloves and coat, and said hello to a surprised Frankie.

"No show in town," said Frankie. "What's this? What brings you to town?"

"We're on our way to Hollywood," Archie explained.

"Going into the movies?" Frankie asked.

"No," Archie said, "but if they want me, they can have me."

With that, he dragged Frankie outside to show him an open touring car loaded down with luggage which was now under a blanket of snow. They laughed together about the trip Archie and his friend had ahead of them on this cold night. Then they had dinner and sat around talking until the wee small hours. And when it was time for the travelers to leave, Frankie gave them four bottles of whisky to ward off pneumonia and other ailments.

That was the last time Frankie ever saw Archie Leach, on that night in 1931. But for years after that, Hollywood celebrities or visiting stage stars would walk into the restaurant to look up Frankie and tell him that Archie had sent them. Of course they didn't use the name Archie Leach. They used the name which the handsome young man with the cleft in his chin adopted when he went to Hollywood—Cary Grant.

Another of the most popular dining places in town is Arnold Orsatti's Pump Room, where the steaks and the Italian specialties are as fine as can be found anywhere in the country. A comparatively young man and a warm and interesting host, Arnold has built his spot into a genuinely classy all-round restaurant which has become a big favorite with many of the Federal judges and state and city political leaders as well as diverse natives with a sound taste in culinary delights.

Aside from the food, the host, the excellent drinks and the intimate, living-room atmosphere, a big reason for its popularity is a big, buxom, hearty Negro woman named DeLloyd McKay who plays the piano and sings. She follows that old local custom, too. She stays in one place. She has been playing here for eight years now, sobbing out torch tunes in a husky, emotional voice, shouting out the blues with rare intensity, turning ballads like "Right in Your Own Backyard" into compelling blues, banging out infectious rhythms on the keyboard—all of this in a way that would make her a sensation if she were in New York, a more spirited edition of Mabel Mercer, perhaps.

She has been playing and singing for a long time—George Gershwin liked the way she did his tunes, in her younger days—and she has been playing and singing here so long that she can go into almost every patron's favorite number the moment he walks in from the bar. It isn't important, but "Sleepy Time Gal" greets me.

This place—and there is now a companion Bonfire Room above

the Pump Room, Arnold having turned his old cafe on the street level into a second classy restaurant—also has a bartender who must be the bettor with the worst luck in the world. His name is Roland Nenno, and he has a perfect straight man behind the bar with him to build up his tales of woe in Primo Taranova.

I'll tell you the kind of hard-luck guy this Roland is. He's the kind of guy who made a bet on St. Louis against the Phillies, went to the game to watch his money come home, and found himself sitting next to a priest—who was rooting for the Phillies. St. Louis was ahead when Roland arrived but, being a good Catholic, he couldn't cheer for the Cardinals. The Phillies rallied.

Roland lost his bet.

In 1956, late in the season, Roland decided to make his first bet on the Phillies. Southpaw Harvey Haddix, with an impressive record, was scheduled to pitch. It looked real good for the Phillies. That was the night something went wrong with Haddix' arm while he was warming up in the bull pen. The arm trouble came too late to change the betting odds, but it did change Roland's chances of winning considerably, even though he didn't have any priest—that he knew about, anyway—going against him this time.

That night the Phillies decided to see if infielder Granny Hamner was a pitcher and sent him in to start the first game of his major league career on the mound. Granny didn't look like a second Bob Feller.

Roland lost the bet.

Roland loves betting and baseball almost as much as that diamond authority and thoroughly nice guy Bill Benson, who has been serving them up at the Essex Hotel bar for years. And, like Bill, he is a good loser. When Roland's wife left him, all that remained in the apartment was the television set and an old orange crate on which he could sit to watch the baseball games.

Roland was happy.

Chapter XIII

The Stories Arrive with the Darkness

ROLAND NENNO's story is the kind you learn about at night. For, if there is no night life in our town as compared to some other towns about the land, this is nevertheless true: It is when evening arrives that spirits grow sad and dreams start to fade. It is when darkness comes that you meet the strange and the tragic, the unusual and bizarre, and some of the more colorful and picturesque people of the world we struggle in.

It is in the nighttime that you run into many stories that linger in the memory long past the next morning and the new day. Sometimes they aren't stories, really. They are simply scenes that somehow stick around for you, perhaps because they tell so much about life in a casual, unannounced and unpretentious way. But the night is always alive with these haunting fragments of life.

One night at a little midtown bar, I remember . . .

The girl and her companion were standing there sipping martinis and engaging in barely audible conversation. The man lowered his voice even more, so that only she could hear it, and started to talk earnestly. She smiled. He reached into his pocket and pulled out the little square box. Grinning like a man who had touched a rainbow, he slipped the ring on her finger. Then he shouted at the bartender happily. "Champagne," he shouted. "Champagne for everybody."

The other bar patrons were the usual bar patrons. Bored. Lonely. Conniving. Planning. Dreaming. Remembering. Hoping for a make. Killing time with a drink. But suddenly the contagion of the moment for the young couple touched them. They shared something of the joy and expectation and big hopes. And they took turns buying drinks for the newly engaged pair for half an hour.

But the young man and his girl finally floated out of the place. The aura of happiness lingered for a few more minutes. Then normalcy took over again and the patrons returned once more to their sophistication, their waiting, their boredom, their loneliness.

Mostly the stories are about people hardly anyone would know. One night I found out about a girl . . .

You could have called her a playgirl in the town—and you would have been right. She never pretended to be anything else. But, in her fashion, she was always true to the dictates of her heart. Not always good, nor always bad. Not always right, nor always wrong.

She played her life out in the bright lights and the gloomy shadows, with a drink and a hangover, courage and fear, a laugh and a tear—hilarious laughter in a crowd mocking the silence of the early morning, and quiet tears in a lonely room. She was about thirty at this time and it was almost the end of the line even then, the joy ride was over, time to get off the roller coaster.

In better days she had been comfortably married. But she was a restless girl, pursuing phantoms of fun that invited her to go places beyond the quiet home. She left her husband, became a hostess at a small bar and depended on the bottle to satisfy her craving for excitement. But finally she looked in the bottle one night and found that all of the pretty sprites had turned into goblins. She decided then to go back to her husband and the better life. She was going to do that right up until an afternoon when she suddenly felt ill and went to a doctor.

So she had stuck to the bottle and life after dark, as I discovered that night. She didn't want to be a burden to her husband. Not when she only had about a year to live.

There are usually names to go with the people, of course, but rarely are they familiar ones to the public at large. One of the most unusual jobholders the town has ever had, for instance, was the lady bouncer at Steve Brodie's Sho-Bar, right in the heart of our Tenderloin. Her name is Mrs. Mary Hoffman and she is an amiable, warmhearted Irish woman who doesn't smoke, doesn't drink and wouldn't harm a fly.

She worked at this tough spot for more than a decade, right up until the night it closed down. That was something like appointing a scoutmaster as the leader of the worst gang of juvenile delinquents in town, but Mrs. Hoffman was well equipped for her rather novel role in the hurly-burly world of business. She wouldn't harm a fly but she never believed in taking anything from anybody, either. She tips the beam at an impressive two hundred pounds or so, distributed equitably over a five-foot ten-inch frame.

One thing that Mrs. Hoffman learned during her years of bouncing uncouth, unruly and uninhibited customers into the street is that the world, up to the present moment, has produced nothing quite so devilish as the drunken woman.

"I can't stand a drunken woman," she told me. "I can humor a drunken man, but not a drunken woman. A man you can reason with. They're easier to handle. But drunken women are the nastiest things going. They start calling you all kinds of names, names you can't take."

Mrs. Hoffman, who was born in the old Swamp-poodle section (around Twenty-ninth Street and Allegheny Avenue), had no special method of giving naughty customers the old heave-ho.

"I don't use any judo," she said, "just what I learned myself. Sometimes it's by the back of the neck. Other times you give them an initial push in the chest. And sometimes you just talk them out. If I can, that's the way I do it."

The technique varied with women, too.

"It just depends on what trouble I'm going to have with a woman," she told me. "Maybe I have to hit her first. Sometimes, with a real tough woman, you do.

"And the first thing they always say is: 'Don't hit me, I'm a lady.' After they've called *you* everything in the book. If they were ladies, they wouldn't use that kind of language!"

Mrs. Hoffman has been married for nearly forty years. "To the same man, too."

He is a bartender, which made it nice for them when she was working at Steve Brodie's because they both finished their jobs at the same hour. When she was at Brodie's he always met her on the corner up the street with their boxer dog Butch and they would walk home together. That was the time of day that Mrs. Hoffman liked best.

Sometimes you don't even know, and never will know, the people whose stories you pick up at night. But you remember them. You remember them for a long time.

I heard this story in one of those spots which attract the younger crowds. Youth was having its fling that night. Not noisily, but quietly and slowly, as though tomorrow would never come. Actually, much of the night had slipped away already for its rendezvous with morning, there were only minutes to count on the day's watch, and the dance music being played by the small band was easy and soft and sentimental, a fitting counterpoint to the scene.

There were some fifteen or sixteen couples on the floor and the girls were pretty, bright-eyed in their youth, playing the role of sophistication pleasantly, escaping adolescence in their frilly evening gowns. Now, their time of triumph moving toward a diary entry, they glided slowly across the floor with their partners, resting heads on shoulders in the prelude to the kiss that would come in a more secluded spot, with the stars as the only spectators. They knew the night was ending, of course. But watching them dance there so calmly, so completely engrossed in each other and the present moment, the boys and girls together, it seemed like the sort of tableau that *could* remain permanent . . . as though tomorrow *would* never come.

I turned my back on romance then and ordered the routine nightcap at the bar beyond the dance floor. My friend lifted his glass and drained his drink and said, "I heard a little story the other day . . ."

He told it casually. It has stuck around in my mind in a rather haunting fashion and the more I think of it the more poignant it becomes, the more solidly it remains in my memory, all of the meanings and implications dancing around the simple incident like mischievous sprites eluding pursuit. It is a story, this tale told at a bar in a late hour, that encompasses many things—love and pride and admiration, and the kind of tragedy that lurks silently in shadows, making no gaudy announcement of its presence in the headlines, not chattering its whereabouts in some busy police court.

Tomorrow *does* come along, the story says . . .

"In my town . . ." my friend said. It is a little town in South Jersey. "In my town there is a married couple I've known for many years. They have been happy together as long as I can remember. They tell me, the older people, that there couldn't have been a more handsome pair. He was a nice-looking guy and she was a pretty little thing . . ."

She was always the gay one, it seemed, the chipper one. And he was happy to be with her. They had lived a lot of years together as man and wife, as good companions, sharing the average joys and average troubles that come along to people in America and everywhere. She was ninety. Her husband was eighty. And they were still in love. They still had a romance, these two. Do you want to know why?

"They have grown old together gracefully," my friend said. "That is, it was that way until just recently."

Then time had taken its inevitable toll and the husband had to watch the wife very carefully. One day the wife left the water running in the kitchen and flooded the floor. Bill (this is the name I will give her husband) scolded her a bit.

His punishment was in her reply. She was in love with her husband, this woman of ninety, and she said to this man who had scolded her:

"Well, I don't know who you are. But if Bill were here, you wouldn't talk to me that way."

That is the little story that has stuck around. I keep thinking of the little ninety-year-old woman, still the loyal wife, still the admirer of her husband, still the lover. I hear her speaking for a lifetime of love and saying: ". . . if Bill were here, you wouldn't talk to me that way." And then I think of the boys and girls together, dancing the night away.

Chapter XIV

Some People Who Came to Our After-Dark Scene

SOMETIMES the names are more familiar ones, like the people who come to town to entertain.

Pee Wee Russell was here.

A year before he arrived he had been lying on a hospital bed in San Francisco, sick, emaciated, broke and just about ready to travel down a long road without the clarinet and the music that have been his life. When his friends from the world of jazz had gone to see the wasted-away man from Okmulgee, Oklahoma, and a hundred smoky clubs, figuring he had blown out his last feverish notes, he had said: "Tell the newspapers not to print any sad stories about me."

So there was no sad story, there didn't need to be, because Pee Wee was around again, up from that bed of pain and pursuing the pleasure that has been his since he was a kid—just playing the kind of music he likes to play.

Pee Wee came to the bandstand at the Rendezvous, long the town's most popular jazz music spot but gone now, its owner Lee Guber busy with his Valley Forge Music Fair and teaching at Penn. Pee Wee was a gaunt figure of a man—like John Carradine, who delivered his eloquent speeches from the same bandstand—a gaunt figure of a man with wrinkled forehead, satchels under his eyes, that familiar brush mustache, a large wide nose—bending almost painfully over the clarinet, it seemed, to find the armies of elusive notes. And he was a happy man again. Not completely well, but what else would he have been doing?

"It's the only thing for me," he said. "It gets in your blood and it stays there. I've never done anything else, never wanted to do anything else.

"I enjoy hearing fellows on their instruments, playing little original ideas. Sometimes it's good, sometimes it's bad.

"Sometimes it comes out right, just the way you figured it, and that makes you feel fine inside. It makes you want to smile or yell, it's so good the way it comes out."

He's probably a pretty tired guy after the life he's lived ("He almost died from too much living," Eddie Condon had explained when he was in the hospital), after all of the long nights and all of the lusty notes. And he was gaunt and thin . . .

"I never weighed much anyway," he said, and went on playing for his happiness.

Lew Jenkins was here.

The last I heard the former lightweight champion was a master sergeant in the Army at Fort MacArthur in San Pedro, California. But when he was here he wasn't sitting on any steady income. He was a hero but he needed some money. Big Bill Rodstein gave Lew a break when Lew was hurting for one and Bill was operating the cafe, the musical bar, that is still called Big Bill's. Lew wasn't much of an act. But let me tell you about Lew . . .

You can have a handy guy like Sande, as the sports writer rhymed many years ago when the famous jockey was booting the winners home. But for my handy man, I'll take a guy with a bashed-in beak and a beat-up body, an easygoing, love-the-world guy name of Lew Jenkins. Lew, a drawling Texan who had considerable fun in his life (he'll tell you frankly that "a bottle of whisky and a motorcycle" cost him his lightweight boxing title) was having fun in town that week. He was getting up on the stage at Big Bill's, all dressed up in the fancy kind of cowboy suit he loves to wear, and strumming a gee-tar and singing some western songs for the people. And every once in a while, during the night, he recited an inspirational piece called "A Deck of Cards."

Now you could have called this corn, I suppose, and paged Eddie Guest—but you wouldn't have when Lew was up there speaking, because when he looked out over the crowd and started to say the good words, the whole business took on a humble kind of beauty, like some ragamuffin kid in a dirty alley gazing up at the stars. And maybe this was the whole tip-off on Lew Jenkins. Here was this guy who had literally been fighting for a living ever since he was a kid, picking up some rootin'-tootin' fun on the side, and he *meant* those words.

He meant that it's a good world and it's full of good people. And he was right proud that he had memorized those words. He was right proud of that recitation, because it was about God and love and goodness.

Sergeant Lew Jenkins—he was a plain old sergeant then—could have been proud of some other things, too, including a Silver Star that he had won over in Korea, when he didn't have to be there. He was on furlough when he came to town. Both the Army and the union had given him the okay to take off his soldier's suit for a week and work at the local spot. This is where he had sung before when he was hungry and couldn't go on with the warfare in the ring any longer. He was through then, through for good after taking a million punches in a hundred foggy fight clubs.

The next week he was due to turn in again and ship to Puerto Rico. And there would be a mess hall over there for an old and battered fighter. Lew would be eating good. And that had always been a worry with him.

When he was a teen-age kid in Texas, he had joined a carnival. "Had to do something to keep eating," he told me. "So I went on this little ole show working the boxing booth. Anybody who could stay two rounds with me got fifty bucks from the boss. Only way for me to keep eating was to keep the boss from giving away fifties. So I beat 'em all. All sizes. Figure I had more than a thousand of those two-rounders. Taught me a lot."

It taught him enough to carry him to the lightweight championship of the world when he knocked out Lou Ambers back in 1940

Manayunk

in a brawl that had the customers yipping like cowboys and Indians.

This is Lew's third hitch in the Army. Before he entered the pro ring, he was with the peacetime forces.

"I became a mess sergeant," he said. "Thataway, I could always be sure of chow."

When World War II broke out, he put away his gloves and joined again. He resumed his mess sergeant status, and saw service in both the ETO and the Philippines. When the Korean action began, he got back into khaki, qualified as a paratrooper, although well into his thirties, and was assigned to the 2nd Division.

And all at once, over in Korea, the kitchen didn't seem a very exciting place. He asked to be assigned as an infantryman.

"I'm not a brave man," he told me that night in Big Bill's, "but you know, I love to be with the underdog. Well, they made me a platoon sergeant, and I got into the rough stuff, all right."

He made it a good fight, too. During the hasty withdrawal from Bloody Ridge, Lew's platoon opened and held a road block for two days, permitting the orderly retreat of an entire battalion. And they gave the old and battered fighter a Silver Star for that, a Silver Star for gallantry in action.

"We just wanted to hold that road open," Lew said with a grin, "so's they could get the field kitchens out."

How can you beat a handy guy like that?

A little guy named Hal Haig was here, too.

He didn't draw many customers either. Here's the way it was with him . . .

Jobs aren't always easy to get when you're walking down the other side of the hill. A guy like Hal Haig stops in at a booking office and the agents take a look at him and they say, "This guy, he's got an act?" See, he's no kid any more, this Hal Haig.

"I'm pushing forty-five," he says. He says it with a smile because he was born, actually, before this century saw the light of day. And, he says ,"I know a lot of agents that won't even book you if you're over *thirty-five*."

Hal Haig is over thirty-five and besides he's a little unimpressive-looking guy. He only weighs about 140 pounds and he's bald and he wears thick glasses. He doesn't look like an entertainer. And so they say, "This guy, he's got an act?"

But let nobody sell the little guy short. Hal Haig may not look like a handsome singer or a daffy comedian or certainly not the star athlete and movie stunt man he once was. But he has an act which includes the Chaz Chase type of pantomime, magic, sleight of hand, chewing cigarettes, balancing, tricks—all adding up to genuinely funny novelty stuff.

And he's got a past, and it's the comfort and joy of his present. When things are tough these days, it's nice to be able to live in the glory of the past. That helps. And let's not sell the little, bald-headed guy short because once he made Keystone Cop comedies for Mack Sennett with Marie Prevost and Gloria Swanson and Polly Moran and Louise Fazenda. He still carries with him their faded pictures along with his tattered newspaper clippings. He was in *Why Worry*, too, with Harold Lloyd, and a lot of other movies back in 1915 and then after World War I. Whenever they needed acrobatic work they called on Haig in those days out in Hollywood.

And once he was on the American Olympic team, the 1920 team that went to Antwerp and also included a young Philadelphia oarsman named John B. Kelly. And once a king, King Albert of Belgium, smiled at him and presented him with a medal because he had won third honors in diving in those Olympic Games. There is more to Hal Haig than meets the eye.

And when you watched him go through his act at Orsatti's, before Arnold turned that little club into a restaurant, maybe you should have known that the little guy with the big smile, the earnest desire to bring laughter into your lives, came from a poor Armenian family named Prieste. He was born in Fresno, California, and the diving ability which carried him to his greatest glory he learned on his own, diving from the wharves in Los Angeles. He earned a lot of medals with his diving skill and he went a lot of places, giving exhibitions in Honolulu and on the Seine River in Paris after the Olympics.

He's been in show business—vaudeville, the circus, burlesque, night clubs—for a lot of years now and he knows there isn't much chance for a guy walking down the other side of the hill.

"But if I could just get to the top . . ." he says.

And he remembers then that fine day when he stood poised gracefully at the top of a diving board in faraway Antwerp, Belgium, a proud young Armenian boy from America, and made the four beautifully executed dives which made his life. He carries with him still a brightly colored poster from those Olympics of 1920, autographed by many members of the American team. He shows it to you proudly.

"It's a beautiful thing, isn't it?" he says.

Sally Rand was here, of course.

Where hasn't that old girl been with her fans? And one night at the old Click, when it was a busy and bustling night spot, I learned how the world's most famous dance began. Or at least this is what I was told by Miss Rand, the lady who left a farm in Hickory County, Missouri, at the age of thirteen to see the world and has been showing herself to the world ever since.

"White birds flying in the moonlight on my grandfather's farm." That was her inspiration. That's what she told me.

"The farm was a swampy place," she went on to explain, "and the big herons migrating South always stopped there. And the moon comes up real early out there, an enormous big harvest moon. When the herons are down you can't see their legs, you know, just the enormous wingspread. It was very affecting to an imaginative girl."

In view of the influence, albeit indirect, which the heron has thus had upon the American entertainment scene, it is worth noting perhaps that the birds which landed on the farm in Missouri are from the family Ardeidae. According to Webster, they have "soft plumage. Some species exhibit dichromatism," Webster points out, "and may develop special plumes in the breeding season." This sort of background knowledge is almost essential if one is to fully appreciate Miss Rand's imaginative dance—if she's still doing it at this late date. The dance is not quite meaningless without the information. But it loses something, maybe the dichromatism.

Another night I ran into one of the first girls to dance with doves. Her name was Narda and she had a twinkle in her words. She said very frankly that there was no symbolism in her dance.

"Actually, in India," she said, "the white dove is sacred, and they perform temple dances there. But I don't know whether they use doves or not."

Narda's research had been more along the lines of what was sure-fire with the American public, or a substantial segment thereof.

"The birds simply add novelty to the act," she explained. "And they also widen the field of interest. After all, women like birds. And a lot of men raise pigeons, as you know." That just about seemed to cover it.

The greatest athlete of them all, Jim Thorpe, just about came to the end of an Indian's trail in our town. It was a long trail to a lot of places, and Jim Thorpe was finally approaching the blind alley at the end of it when he played Orsatti's Cafe (now the Bonfire Room) with a cheap Indian show. Arnold Orsatti gave him a break because he had always admired the big Indian as an athlete and wanted to help him out. Jim Thorpe needed money.

And this, I remember, is the way it was that night he opened . . .

Standing around the bar, they sipped their drinks slowly and waited with silent partners named Boredom for the show to begin. Mostly they were middle-aged and rather tired-looking, a cross section of the people at a lot of bars on a dreary fall evening, heavy with the threat of rain.

A blond girl looking for somebody named Company turned to the bespectacled man next to her and asked, for the sake of meaningless conversation. "Who'd you come to see?"

His expression remained a drab still life. He mentioned the name. "Who?" said the blonde.

A sailor standing close to his girl, in the manner of the gob at the bar, craned his neck toward a corner of the room and said, "There he is."

"Yeah," the girl agreed and drained her glass of beer and looked for the bartender.

(He was born in a place called Prague, Oklahoma, in 1888 and they called him Chief Bright Path and, although the Indian boy didn't know it, there was to be a Glory Road ahead, and then that long lane they tell about.

He went to the Carlisle Institute when he was fifteen and one day he looked at the high jump bar, which had been left at five feet eight inches. "That bar doesn't seem very high," he said. "Did you ever high jump?" asked the other boy. "Not over a bar," the answer was. "But if a horse can do it, I can."

And he took off his heavy shoes and jumped and cleared the bar by four inches and Pop Warner saw him do it—and he became an athlete.)

The elderly, white-haired gentleman had been at the bar for a couple of hours, waiting. "I saw in the paper that he was going to be here and I wanted to see him again," this husky gentleman said. His name was Jim Flower, he lived in Fairlawn, New Jersey, and he was an executive with the U.S. Rubber Co. But once he had played end on a great Ohio State team and later in the twenties he had played with Akron when the boy who grew up to be the Big Guy was with the Canton Bulldogs.

"He was the greatest player who ever put on a uniform," Flower said.

"Everybody says that," Flower was told.

Flower grinned, "Yeah," he said, "but I had to tackle him." And he fondled a pleasant old memory in his smile.

"When's he go on?" a girl asked her date. "I wish he'd go on and get it over with."

(On this November day in 1911, the Big Guy had already kicked three fields goals for the Carlisle Indians against Harvard. The score was tied, 15 to 15, though. Carlisle had the ball, fourth down, only a couple of minutes to go. His leg was battered and bandaged from a previous game, but he calmly stepped back and kicked the winning goal from the Harvard 48-yard line.

And a year later against powerful Army he took a punt on the 10-yard line and raced and twisted his way 50 yards for a touchdown. But his team was offside. So Army kicked again and this time he had to go 95 yards for the touchdown. The Indians won the game, 27 to 6.)

Princess Louisa, an entertainer about town, stepped to the mike on the stage in the rear of the room, cloudy with smoke and loud with talk. She was wearing an abbreviated costume in the Indian motif with the international appeal.

"A man whom you all know," she said. "He has done everything better than any other man has. I'd like to present . . ."

The Big Guy came forward and stood in the spotlight, still a rugged and impressive figure, with a face worn by time and experience into an unforgettable portrait.

"It is wonderful being here and back in the City of Brotherly Love—I hope," he said, grinning a bit self-consciously. And he introduced the Thunderbird Troupe, refugees from a fair grounds. A wild and shouting dance began. "Yeeowah yeeowah!" And there were bursts of laughter from the bar.

(They tell of the time Knute Rockne first tackled him in a pro game. The Big Guy patted Rockne on the back and said: "That was a great tackle, Mr. Rockne. But you don't understand. All these folks came out here to see old Jim run."

On the next play the Big Guy went around Rockne's end again and dashed 60 yards for a touchdown. Rockne, hit hard, was still staggering around when the Big Guy came up, patted him once more on the back, and said: "Thanks, Mr. Rockne, I knew you'd let 'em see old Jim run.")

As each of the Indian performers imported from New York took a turn, the Big Guy stood at the side of the stage, stiff and erect and smiling—introducing first and then almost sheepishly starting the applause. "And now Sunbeam is going to tell you why she left Arizona . . . And now Princess Louisa will sing you a song . . . And now we will have another performance by Smiling Bear . . ."

As Smiling Bear went into another Hopi dance, the press agent was smitten by an idea. Tomorrow, he said, he would buy a cigar store Indian and put it out front. The press agent was pleased with the sudden thought, and happy.

(In baseball he was a picture in the field, running crazily to grab a fly ball, emulating a deer on the basepaths. It was a minor sport for him, and yet he played with McGraw's New York Giants.

They said he couldn't hit a curve ball but he hit them often enough to bat .364 in the Eastern League in 1919.

In track meets he would rarely win less than seven events. And in the 1912 Olympics at Stockholm, Sweden, he became the first man ever to win both the pentathlon and the decathlon.

He stepped before King Gustav of Sweden after those fantastic performances, this young man who had just tucked world fame in his back pocket.

And said the King to the young man from Oklahoma:

"You, sir, are the greatest athlete in the world.")

"Well folks, this is the end of the show," the Big Guy said. "Did you enjoy the show?"

And the bored and the tired at the bar applauded, perfunctorily. Not for the show, really, but for the Big Guy's past, his days of glory. Not for the emcee in the Indian headdress but for a field goal booted in 1911 and a race run, hurdles jumped, weight thrown, in Stockholm, Sweden, in 1912.

(They took the medals away. He made some Western movies. He gave some lectures. He dug some ditches. And it was a long lane and you needed some money and you got a job and you introduced some acts and you thanked some people for coming to see you, for remembering . . .)

"Thank you very much," said Jim Thorpe, the Big Guy, and he stepped down from the stage and went to a table in the corner, walking erectly, a rugged and impressive figure in a fancy Indian outfit.

Not too long after that night he died, leaving a little money and a lot of legends behind him. It would have been fitting if he had died in a football stadium or on a baseball field or on a cinder track, for these were the scenes of his glory and everything after them was anticlimax. But when death came to the tired old man who had been called Chief Bright Path as a boy in Oklahoma, he was living in a trailer.

And I remembered, when he died, that last night I had seen him. He had acquired fame by the handfuls but there was no cash on hand at the moment. And it had been an infinitely sad night. The world's greatest athlete, no javelin to throw, no football to kick, was the world's worst emcee. He didn't have a gag in his bag of introductions. And there was nothing funny about his being there. He needed money and he wanted to earn it. And the days of his performances were ended. He was there as a sight to see—like the Grand Canyon or a flea circus.

He didn't know any dance steps. He had done other things in that stadium in Stockholm. Later on he had dug ditches. But he had never learned dancing in between the glory and that kind of grave. And he didn't have any songs to sing.

A few people came in to see him that sad and rainy night out of curiosity, and the numbers grew as the week went on. But I don't think anybody really cared except that white-haired gentleman named Jim Flower. In a way, the two of them shared a memory that opening night and they were the only ones who could, because of all the years that had gone by since Jim Thorpe had the world at his feet—before it bounced up and, as it has a habit of doing, kicked him in the teeth.

From the table where Jim Thorpe sat with his memories that night to the stage where he acted as emcee was only a few steps. But it is one of the longest, toughest hauls in the book—from Glory Road to Nowhere. And yet Jim Thorpe, the big Indian from Oklahoma, who had once conquered a world of sport, was a proud guy that night. And proudly, I am sure, proudly he died —in the trailer that had become his home, at the end of an Indian's long, long trail.

Chapter XV

Nobody Needs a Calendar Here

IN PHILADELPHIA nobody needs a calendar to know it's spring. There are too many other ways to tell that the season's here. The sun gets brighter, the evenings grow longer. The children, coming out of their winter hibernation, shout louder, run faster, laugh harder. The woodlands in Fairmount Park and on all of the outskirts of our big town start to apply their colorful make-up and pretty up for their annual big date with summer.

The young lovers, schoolbooks under their arms, start to stroll on the tree-lined Parkway and to talk in soft, meaningful voices on the benches along that wide, tire-humming drive from the midtown business establishments past the culture spots—the Philadelphia Museum of Art, the main branch of the Free Library, the Franklin Institute, the Academy of Natural Sciences. And their whispers are in the air.

The old men who look like scholars come out of their musty, dusty, broken-down rented rooms after the long cold months to browse through the musty, dusty, broken-covered tomes at the open-air bookstalls in the alleyway beside Leary's Book Store.

Families start to gather in Fairmount Park on the Sundays

which hold the promise of summer, and baseball grounds and softball grounds and tennis courts in that green city paradise are bustling with fresh-limbed activities.

The oars start to dip through the placid waters of the Schuylkill, whose shores are dotted with the quarters of all the old boating clubs (Boat House Row, it is called), and the sculls glide gracefully under the bridges across the river.

The Phillies, those fabulous Whiz Kids of 1950 who won a pennant when nobody expected them to and then, alas, became the Fizz Kids, come home from the South and the leather lungs begin their bellowing from Connie Mack Stadium, which was once—for many years—Shibe Park and was then renamed for a long, lean man they called Mr. Baseball and the Grand Old Man of Baseball. And the old-timers almost expect to see the ramrod figure in the dugout, pointing to an outfielder with his scoreboard, because he had been there for so many, many years.

The girls put on their sweaters and fairly burst with growing up. The traffic cops seem more lenient. They will even listen if you tell them you didn't notice the sign, didn't see the light, thought you had gotten through on caution. And even the bums have a spring in their step. No calendar is needed to tell us that the season for a sigh has arrived in our town.

A couple of young lovers told me it was spring one year. They were walking out the Parkway together in the evening time. He wasn't the least bit handsome, and she wasn't the least bit beautiful. Both of them wore heavy horn-rimmed glasses. They carried books under their arms and they were obviously the bookish types. They had been talking earnestly and seriously. Then suddenly they stopped talking, stopped walking, and turned to each other and kissed. And they looked at each other, then, as though he were the most handsome guy in the world and she were the most beautiful girl in the world. And he was—to her! And she was—to him! And there was nothing, there is nothing, in all of the books that they will ever study which could really explain that. Only spring!

Another year I learned it was spring at Leary's, because even that old bookstore isn't going to sell young love short in the springtime. Leary's, of course, is a Philadelphia landmark.

In our town you may buy jewelry at Caldwell's or Bailey, Banks & Biddle's or Kind's. You may go shopping for everything from bedroom furniture to chocolate candy at the John Wanamaker store (with its organ music in the court, a rendezvous for hundreds of shoppers day after day) or alert, progressive Gimbels or Strawbridge & Clothier's (the department store with two of the most esteemed names in town) or busy Lit Brothers or recently remodeled Snellenburgs.

You may go shopping for clothes, if you are milady, at The Blum Store or Bonwit Teller's or Nan Duskin's or Lord & Taylor's on City Line or any of the new suburban branches of the older, well-known stores or, if you are poorer, Blauner's. You may buy your stationery at Decker's, and your sports goods at Pearson's, and your men's clothing at Jacob Reed's, and rugs here and shoes there.

You may buy your new books at the department stores, which have well-stocked book departments, or at any of the smaller shops —the inviting Charles Sessler's, or Bains', or Balis', or Whitman's, or Womrath's, or Doubleday, or Fireside, or Frigate, or the new Cefra.

But if you want an old book or a rare book or a textbook or an unusual book, you go to Leary's and there is no "may" about it. You go to Leary's. Period.

It is a store with a homely, humble front, two sidewalk stands with books usually selling for a dime, and a reading gold mine for an interior. And it has been a word for all the many wonders in printed pages ever since it was founded in 1836 by William A. Leary. Here browsing is almost as applauded as buying. The late Robert G. Hoag, who died in 1956 at seventy-three after a fifty-six-year association with the firm—Philadelphians like to stay in one place; they do not move around a lot—once said:

"Of course we like them to buy, but we want them to browse around, and we never want to bother any of them."

Well, browse they do, and for many rich hours. Here, too, at this old landmark in the town booklovers from all over the world can inscribe their names and home addresses in a big book—looking for all the world like an old Uriah Heep ledger—at the front of the store to indicate that they have made the pilgrimage.

Beside this book is a stack of post cards showing the familiar storefront. Visitors are invited to fill out a card to the folks at home or friends far away, write a message, and turn the card over to Leary's for prompt mailing. One spring day, the spring I am talking about, a book collector from Toronto, Canada, wrote his name in the book. A short time later a romantic young lady spotted the address, copied it off on one of the cards, added her own message, and left her card for mailing.

"Dear Sir," she wrote. "I am twelve and extremely beautiful. I would be glad to hear from you in Toronto." She then signed her name and a local address.

The love note was found in the box for all of the cards. Now ordinarily, in accord with the store policy, her card would have been examined and tossed casually into oblivion. In this case, it was duly stamped and forwarded to the unsuspecting book collector in Toronto.

There could have been many explanations for this strange act, I suppose. Sellers of old books are supposed to be suspended in a benign state of mind, to start with. Somebody could have been wandering in a field of philosophy. Somebody, some girl in the store, was thinking of a young man combining the appeal of Tab Hunter, James Dean, Tony Curtis and Marlon Brando. Somebody, some man in the store, was thinking of a girl made up of equal parts of Anita Ekberg, Sophia Loren, Audrey Hepburn and Lana Turner. Somebody was watching Stan Musial hit a triple with three men on base. Somebody had just found a million bucks. Somebody had just been touched by Dame Fame.

It could have been any number of things. But there was really only one true, genuine and incontrovertible explanation. It was spring, ladies and gentlemen!

Chapter XVI

The Theory Being "It Pays to Advertise"

VISIT PHILADELPHIA THIS SPRING

For the young in heart, a trip to the Quaker City is an adventure. Here are bright lights, matchless entertainment, historic shrines, and much more. See a city on the march, where progress blends uniquely with tradition. For a metropolitan vacation, Philadelphia is unexcelled for luxury, gaiety and excitement.

That's what the cover of an official and attractive folder put out by the city says.

Now I grant you that a tendency to exaggerate is apparent there. Philadelphia *is* excelled by other cities for luxury and for gaiety and for excitement. Its entertainment can be matched *and* surpassed by numerous other cities. But it does have the historic shrines, it is on the march and progress does, very definitely, blend with tradition in the town. And if you add everything up, it does have as much to offer the vacationer as any other city.

A touch of boasting has to be allowed an official city talking about itself in an official capacity. And here is the significant aspect of this folder called "Philadelphia in the Spring": It reflects the new and modern and advertising-style program to sell the city.

Selling Philadelphia to the public, to the nation, to convention planners, has become a big business under the present Democratic administration, which has realized that the town does need a tonic for many phases of its business, particularly its midtown stores (hurt by the migration to the suburbs and parking and traffic problems), its hotels, and its restaurants.

"Visit Philadelphia This Spring," the folder urges. And in the winter and in the summer and in the fall, too, other folders say. For there is one for each season of the year. The first of these folders produced by the Office of the City Representative (Fredric R. Mann is the City Representative and Abe S. Rosen is his Deputy and the busy detail man in the office) came out in the fall of 1956. The one for the spring of 1957 was one fold larger. More than 100,000 of these are distributed about the country through chambers of commerce, airlines, and automobile clubs. The local hotels also distribute them to patrons and the Convention and Visitors Bureau hands out hundreds of them by mail and by direct contact.

The folders refer inquiries about restaurants and other facilities to the Mayor's Office of Information and Complaints and the Convention and Visitors Bureau. The bureau itself publishes a little guide to the town's dining places, hotels, entertainment spots and sports events. Additionally, in the summer of 1957 a new booklet called "The New Philadelphia" was published by the Office of the City Representative. It points up the historical, educational and cultural factors providing Philadelphia with an appeal to the visitor and also stresses the plans for a better city, emphasizing activities around Penn Center, Independence Mall and other improvement projects.

The spring folder first listed eight spots "where history was made" and which are only "a short walk from major hotels." One of those included I have not mentioned thus far in the book. It is the Edgar Allan Poe House at 530 North Seventh Street, where the brilliant but sorely troubled poet and story writer penned "The Raven." (Another great literary figure, Walt Whitman, spent many more years of life across the river in Camden, where the largest hotel bears his name. The newest bridge across the Delaware was also named in his honor.)

A valuable part of these city folders, incidentally, is the fact that telephone numbers are listed for virtually every item mentioned, so that a visitor can make prompt contact with the places of interest.

Following the list of historic spots in the spring folder, there was the suggestion that you "Salute the Glorious 4th" in town. "How better to celebrate Independence Day than in Philadelphia, where American liberty was born?" It's true, in case you've thought of it, that July the Fourth doesn't arrive in the spring. But those crafty City Hall pitch men aren't overlooking a trick. And each folder published attempts to tie in the next one by highlighting some event that will be taking place in the following season of the year. And that's salesmanship for you.

Following the summer pitch was a list of historic churches in the midtown—for any season. A visit to City Hall was then suggested. "The nineteenth century structure, a rare example in America of good French Renaissance-style architecture," the folder said, "is a storehouse of wonder for the curious and adventuresome." Well, there are some natives who might dispute that. But: "Always popular is the splendid view from Billy Penn's tower . . ." No dispute about that.

The folder offered a telephone number to contact for arranging tours of the port, the International Airport, etc. It listed "Ideal Spots for Family Visiting," and some of these I have not mentioned. Here is the complete list:

American Swedish Historical Museum at 1900 Pattison Avenue.

Atwater Kent Museum at 15 South Seventh Street.

Bartram Park Gardens at Fifty-fourth and Eastwick.

Free Library at Nineteenth and the Parkway.

Germantown Historical Society at 5214 Germantown Avenue.

Morris House at 5442 Germantown Avenue (where George Washington lived in 1793–94).

National Philatelic Museum at Broad and Diamond streets.

Pennsylvania Academy of the Fine Arts at Broad and Cherry streets.

Philadelphia Art Alliance at 251 South Eighteenth Street.

Print Club at 1614 Latimer Street.

U. S. Mint at Sixteenth and Spring Garden streets.

U. S. Naval Base at League Island.

University Museum at Thirty-third and Spruce streets.

Times open, visiting hours, telephone numbers were listed to make arrangements easier for the visitor.

There was a listing of exhibits at the Trade and Convention Center, including the permanent Philadelphia Panorama (the town past and present), and of conventions and shows set for newly air-conditioned Convention Hall. Musical and other cultural events were also listed. There were guides to the public golf courses, boating facilities, tennis courts, fishing in the parks, picnics in the parks.

There was a listing of sports events, including the sixty-third annual Penn Relays, always one of the highlights of the athletic year in the town. More than 3,000 college and schoolboy track and field competitors participate in this two-day affair sponsored by the University of Pennsylvania. It has been the world's largest track meet for years.

Places to go in Fairmount Park were described thusly:

"Academy of Natural Sciences . . . Animals and birds in lifelike displays . . .

"Aquarium . . . Visitors see nearly 4,000 live specimens of sea life through glass-walled tanks . . . Schuylkill River below the Art Museum . . . [An error there, gentlemen of City Hall. You don't need "river" with Schuylkill. The word Schuylkill includes river.]

"Fels Planetarium . . . Heavenly bodies are projected on to the domed auditorium ceiling during narrated programs . . . In Franklin Institute . . .

"Franklin Institute . . . Action exhibits include an operating locomotive . . . [And much, much else—this should not be missed by any visitor. It's fascinating, folks.]

"Historic Mansions . . . These lovely structures preserve the spirit of gracious Colonial living . . .

"Museum of Art . . . Here is one of the nation's largest and finest art collections . . .

"Rodin Museum . . . Many of the famous sculptor's finest pieces comprise the entire collection . . .

"Zoological Garden . . . More than 1,800 mammals, birds and reptiles are on exhibit, many in natural surroundings . . ."

Visiting hours, telephone numbers, prices (if any) are given.

The folder concluded with a listing of the central city churches and the hotels. And what it didn't contain, it guided the visitor to with telephone numbers. It didn't miss much, I assure you, and these seasonal folders are helpful to any visitor. Merely to have all of the telephone numbers at hand is a wonderful convenience for the stranger in town. In case you want it, the telephone number of the City Representative's office, which puts out these handy folders, is:

MUnicipal 6–9700. Extension 943. That's just in case you can't find a folder and want to know where to get one.

In addition to these official city folders, there are a number of guides on the newsstands and in the hotels. They provide the routine information and point the way to the regular ports of call. But perhaps there are a few tips to out-of-towners which I can pass on.

Let's see . . . well . . .

The Zoo is a must if you have children. The kiddies are also fascinated by the sun and the moon and the planets and the stars in the Fels Planetarium. If you're a lover of the arts, both the Museum of Art and the Academy of the Fine Arts are musts. Older folks will want to hear the organ music in the John Wanamaker store. There are more famous sites, but there is none more movingly suggestive of the past than the old Christ Church graveyard.

If you are in town in the good old summertime, you shouldn't leave before attending a concert in the sylvan surroundings of the Robin Hood Dell. Theatergoers will find a wide variety of summer attractions at the Playhouse in the Park, right in Fairmount Park, and the nearby Valley Forge Music Fair, Camden County Music Fair, Bucks County Playhouse, St. John Terrell's Lambertville Music Circus and the Brandywine Music Box. The Philadelphia area is probably the busiest summer tent territory in the nation. In past years none of the regular legitimate theaters in the midtown have remained open, but the Erlanger is now air-conditioned.

The Benjamin Franklin Hotel is the nearest to the historic

shrines. The new Sheraton and the old Bellevue-Stratford are the two largest centrally located ones—that is, closest to City Hall. If your activities are going to be centered in West Philly (around Convention Hall, Franklin Field, the Palestra, the Arena), then the Penn Sherwood is the best located hostelry for you.

The Naval Base is well worth a visit, if you want to make the arrangements (Secuity Department, HOward 5-1000, Extension 2915). And you might be the type that gets a big kick out of just watching all of the trains being loaded and unloaded on Delaware Avenue down at the water front.

Almost anybody would be intrigued by Weil's Curiosity Shop at 20 South Second Street, which isn't mentioned in the guidebooks. It's a mecca for visitors with a taste for the bizarre and a landmark known to antiquarians all over the world. Here you will likely find such a varied assortment of items as ancient dueling pistols, tiger skins, high-wheel bicycles, buffalo heads, old ship fittings, snowshoes, sleighs, flintlocks, stuffed owls, mummified arms, and almost any other relic or curio. At one time the place had a chariot to show you. All of this stuff (I think the word is acceptable here) is stored in the shop and four full warehouses. The old shop was operated for nearly fifty years by Benjamin Weil, a puckish little man with ruddy cheeks, who died in December 1956.

You'll find that the cabdrivers know how to get to almost any place. They can also give you some tips on the best eating places. If you like the best food and realize it's not going to be cheap, you shouldn't leave town without trying Orsatti's Pump Room, the Saxony, Frankie Bradley's, the Sans Souci, the Capri, the Warwick, the Barclay, the evening *smörgåsbord* at the Benjamin Franklin, and a couple of the sea-food places. All of these, except possibly the latter—depending on which one you choose—are in the midtown. Some are rather high in price. For kosher and dairy foods, you should make a trip to the Blintza, and for kosher foods of all kinds, the Bain's cafeteria restaurants are outstanding, with delectable dishes at reasonable prices. You'd probably get a boot out of a sandwich at Moe's Luncheonette on South Ninth Street. Moe just expanded. His number used to be only 108½. But the onetime "hole-in-the-wall" (always busy) now has a complete number

—108. You should try a mammoth hot dog at Levis'. The cabbie knows where it is. If you want hard-shelled crabs at any time of the year, you go to Snockey's Oyster and Crab House. Again, it's best just to hop into a cab.

Take a cab to Connie Mack Stadium, too, if you want to watch the Phillies play baseball or the Eagles play football. Naturally it costs more than the PTC, but the visitor could find the slow and cheaper way a bit distressing. After the games, you'll find it tough to get a cab. The cabs in town stay away from big events because they get tied up in traffic and lose time. That's no excuse, but that's the way it is. Your best bet after the game is to walk to Broad Street and grab the subway or a bus into town there.

If you want to know what seamier events went on in town the night before, you might attend the morning police court hearings at the Twelfth and Pine streets station. Don't park illegally. The police give out tickets with gusto. The last couple of years, in fact, they have been trying to make prescribed quotas. And you'll pay the fine unless you know a committeeman.

There are Dow-Jones stock tickers in the Coach Room at the Warwick Hotel and at Big Bill Rodstein's Latimer Cafe—if you want to check your investments while guzzling a few.

If you're in town in the summertime, by all means get an air-conditioned hotel room. Our town has a lot of places to visit and a lot of sights to see. But it does get hot and humid, and you'll want some comfort in your room when you get back from the sticky streets. Any questions?

Chapter XVII

Additional Potpourri about the Town

Now here I have come this far in the book and I haven't even mentioned the skyscraper situation in our big city. Well, frankly, we're minor league compared to New York. But there are some tall ones for the folks from the country to crane their necks at when they come to town.

The highest structure of all is the Philadelphia Saving Fund (add Society to that and it becomes PSFS to all Philadelphians) Building, which soars into the sky for 491 feet. There are 32 floors of offices topped by an observation tower, making 36 stories in all. It is located at the busy corner of Twelfth and Market streets.

Next is the Philadelphia National Bank Building, which has 25 stories and is 475 feet high. The Girard Trust Building on South Penn Square goes up for 450 feet and is followed by the Lewis Tower at 400 feet. And that winds up the structures over the 400-foot mark.

The Fidelity-Philadelphia Trust Building is 377 feet high, the Penn Mutual Life is 375 feet. And then a non-office building finally climbs into the picture for the first time. It is the Drake Hotel, the figures are 30 stories and 365 feet.

Another office structure, the 364-foot Medical Tower Building, is next and it is followed by The Inquirer Building and the Packard Building, both at 340 feet. Others with heights of more than 300 feet are the Land Title, the Edison, the Architects, 1500 Walnut, the Chateau Crillon, and 1616 Walnut.

All of these are considerably higher than the town's first skyscraper, which was the Betz Building on the southeast corner of Broad Street and South Penn Square. It took two years (from 1891 to 1893) to build that one, and it had 13 stories and was 212 feet high.

The town's been growing upward as well as outward.

Nor have I talked sufficiently about those fabulous Phillies of 1950, who were managed to the team's first pennant since 1915 by quiet-spoken Eddie Sawyer.

Aside from the joyful days when wars came to an end or armistices were celebrated, I don't think the town has ever been so excited and happy as it was on that late Sunday afternoon when the Whiz Kids clinched the pennant in Ebbets Field on Dick Sisler's homer, Richie Ashburn's throw, and Robin Roberts' stout-hearted pitching.

That was the last day of the season and there were those who said that the Phillies, caught up in a losing streak through September, had backed into the flag, had been a lucky club. If anything, it was the reverse of that for this young and gritty Cinderella team. The Whiz Kids lost their No. 2 pitcher, southpaw Curt Simmons, to Uncle Sam for the entire last month. That would be a blow to any team fighting for a pennant. Andy Seminick was running around on an ankle nobody else could have played on. Bill (Swish) Nicholson was hurt and there were other injuries that hampered the team.

But they won anyway. And then they took a bad rap on the World Series, too. Sure, they lost it in four straight to the New York Yankees. But each game was a close one. None was high scoring. And that vaunted Yankee slugging power was really held down by the tired Phillies' pitchers.

Bespectacled Jim Konstanty, the player of the year, the bull pen ace extraordinary, almost beat them and he hadn't even started a game all year. Roberts almost beat them and he was dead tired from a grueling season of many innings on the mound. And even old Ken Heintzelman, the smooth southpaw who was at the end of the baseball trail, almost beat them, although he had won only a few games during the regular season.

It was a great team, when you look at all the angles—its youth, the tough breaks, the fact that it wasn't supposed to go anywhere at all that season. And it made Philly a mighty happy town.

I have come this far and I haven't mentioned the fact that almost everybody has met somebody under "the Eagle" in the John Wanamaker store at one time or another . . . Or the many cultural activities of the busy Art Alliance members, who are always presenting art exhibitions or lectures or readings—or something to stimulate the mind . . . I haven't mentioned the "river wards" with their many phantom voters (the derelicts), who helped roll up the Republican majority for so many elections . . . Or the fact that Philadelphia will support any big musical that comes to town but has a tendency to avoid straight dramas unless they are by Tennessee Williams or have some of his sex stuff in them . . . Or that the Army-Navy game brings the most notables and the biggest-spending crowd to town each year . . . Or that the annual Boy Scout National Jamboree at Valley Forge uses up some half a million eggs and about 560,000 quarts of milk during the week in the summertime when the youngsters cavort on the historic grounds.

I haven't mentioned the power which organized labor holds and the leading part it plays in politics in the town. Some indication of this was given early in 1957 when the Democrats, who have had the most solid support from labor, finally decided not to slate Common Pleas Court Judge Joseph L. Kun for renomination on their ticket. In making that decision, the party leaders were ignoring the desire of one of the party's financial giants, Albert M. Greenfield. The principal reason for it was that the Democrats knew labor was dead set against Judge Kun and didn't want to lose labor's support in the election.

Leary's Book Store

Nor have I mentioned such people as Eddie Gottlieb, who is Mr. Basketball in the town, owner and former coach of the professional Warriors, before that long associated with the Sphas. Temple's smart basketball coach, Harry Litwack, who has been on the court scene almost as long . . . Jumbo Jim Elliott, Villanova's great track coach, whose Wildcats won the A.A.U. indoor crown in 1957—only the third college team in sports history to do that—as well as the NCAA and IC4A titles . . . The late, longtime police official with the catchy nickname, Shooey Malone . . . And fun-loving businessman Danny Friedman and Al Bateoff.

Other popular, well-known, or interesting Philadelphians are veteran Judges Gerald F. Flood, Vincent A. Carroll, John A. Boyle, Eugene V. Alessandroni and Robert V. Bolger. Veteran political powers in the GOP Mort Witkin and Bill Meade, who was seriously wounded in a still unsolved shooting mystery . . . That clever and picturesque attorney, Jake Kossman, who knows the law books so fantastically well . . . William F. B. Koelle, whose clubs are his hobbies . . . Sam Silber, co-owner of the departed Embassy Club, known as "the Mustache"—and a fancy one it is, too. His mild-mannered partner at that spot, Herb Smiler, disliked by nobody . . . Nice guy Mort Berry, public relations man for the Phillies . . . The late Bob Geasey who did the same job for Temple University . . . And veteran band leader Joe Frasetto, who has been a club fixture for many seasons with his violin and his baton.

Our goodhearted Sheriff, Bill Lennox, is another of the real nice guys in town. So is Police Captain Joe Cunnane, of the Accident Investigation Squad, one of the able officers who has come up through the ranks. Then there is that familiar figure in the clubs, Leo DeMayo, who goes wherever there is Latin-American music, dances the *rumba* or the tango with any available partner, acts like a regular and suave member of cafe society—and actually is the doorman at the CR Club. For years before that he was a bellhop at the old Ritz-Carlton Hotel, once one of the ritziest in town, now a thing of the past.

Veteran crime reporter Ralph Cropper, of the *Inquirer*, is a colorful character and a fighting little gamecock of a man, who, I am sure, is going to demand admission to Heaven by showing his press card. He's been everywhere else with it through many moons of labor in the city rooms. And if St. Peter stops him, St. Peter will be the first.

And don't forget Father Divine, whose headquarters are in town . . . Or NBC vice president Manie Sacks, who staged the stormy wedding of Frank Sinatra and Ava Gardner in his home town and remains loyal to all of his old Philly friends . . . Popular wholesale druggist Sol Turnoff . . . Rising young lawyer Jerry Shestack and his wife, Marciarose . . . Barbara Wilson, who must be the prettiest play reviewer in the land . . . Veteran bartenders like Teddy Reginato and Howard Coughlin . . . Lillian Reis, who was the No. 1 chorus girl in town for half a dozen seasons, is now the mother of two children, and operates the intimate little bar on the second floor of the Celebrity Room. And all of my friends who were with the 278th Field Artillery Battalion.

Disc jockey Bill Mercer, who has always wanted to be a writer. This young Negro friend of mine used to work all day at the Aviation Supply Depot and then, to supplement his income and thus provide more completely for his family, he worked at nights—until two o'clock in the morning—at the Latin Casino. I first met him when he was reading *Walden* in the men's room at that club. He was the men's room attendant there. The radio career—and it should be a successful one—came later. It was, naturally, the result of hard work and extra effort.

Janine Mermet, who is the most attractive chorus girl at the moment (she's in the Celebrity Room line). She's really Mrs. Frank Lazos, a busy housewife and the mother of three small children. That's when she isn't dancing. It's hardly the life she envisioned when she met a romantic American G.I. from Schuylkill Haven, Pennsylvania, on a subway train in Paris, France, back in 1946. But you don't raise children on peanuts these days, there is nothing unusual about both husband and wife laboring for the family treasury in our present age, and Janine is happy with her life. "It ees pretty hard," she told me once, "because I take care of the children all day long. But we have fun. We enjoy ourselves." Janine misses Paris. "It has everything," she said. "But I would not like to live there. I like it very much here in Philadelphia. The people, they are very friendly and very helpful."

Former Sheriff Austin (Aus) Meehan, long-time GOP power,

who looks like the politician in every political cartoon—and has a legion of loyal friends who have sworn by him for years . . . And there are famous Penn trackmen of old like Ted Meredith, Barney Berlinger (now a big game hunter), Earl Eby and Billy Carr . . . As well as tennis champ Vic Seixas.

Benedict Gimbel, Jr., president of radio station WIP, first-nighter, host to Bob Hope when the comedian comes to Philadelphia, and one of the more unusual and colorful characters in our town. A man with a mischievous sense of humor, Ben surrounds two pretty and efficient secretaries, Grace Collins and Betsey Coste (incidentally, WIP has more pretty girls per square inch than any business firm in town), with THIMK signs and a raft of slogan cards which offer such lofty and high-minded messages as:

"Minds Are Like Parachutes—They Won't Function Unless Open."

"Co-operation Costs So Little and Accomplishes So Much."

"The Most Underdeveloped Territory in America Is under Men's Hats."

"When It Is Finally Settled That the Thing Is Impossible, Watch Some Fellow Do It!"

"Oh Lord! Help Me To Keep My Big Mouth Shut until I Know What I'm Talking About."

"Blessed Is the Man Who Does Not Bellyache."

"Organization Is the Art of Getting Men to Respond Like Thoroughbreds. When You Cluck to a Thoroughbred, He Gives You All the Speed, Strength of Heart and Sinew in Him . . . When You Cluck to a Jackass, He Kicks."

I don't know where the man gets them. Nor do Gracie and Betsey. Sometimes, I suppose, they wish they did.

Somebody's always getting a plaque from some organization in Philadelphia, usually in return for a free speech or—if the person being honored is a national show business or sports headliner—merely a personal appearance. It boosts attendance at the meetings and is always good for at least a two-paragraph story in the newspapers, thus bringing the organization some publicity.

Those plaques are, as the old phrase has it, a dime a dozen. But there are some awards in the award-giving town which do amount to something. They are, in short, well worth getting, not because of any cash that goes with them but because they are a high honor bestowed upon a distinguished citizen for significant achievement in some field of human progress or human relations.

First among these probably is the Philadelphia Award, established in 1921 through a gift from the late Edward W. Bok. It is presented to the person in the area who during the previous year has contributed some action or service "calculated to advance the best and larger interests of Philadelphia."

It has gone in the past to such diversified personalities as Dr. Russell H. Conwell, Philadelphia Orchestra conductor Leopold Stokowski (the first recipient), Chief Justice Owen J. Roberts, lawyer George Wharton Pepper, Dr. Chevalier Jackson (who developed the bronchoscope), Friends' leader Dr. Clarence E. Pickett, Dr. Thomas S. Gates, industrialist William R. Batt, philanthropist Samuel S. Fels (whose Fels Planetarium is now a part of Franklin Institute), Fellowship House leader Marjorie Penney, former Mayor Clark and concert artist Marian Anderson.

The award includes a medal and a gift of $10,000. After Miss Anderson received the award, she established with the money an award of her own in 1941. The Marian Anderson Award provides scholarships that enable young singers to continue their vocal educations. Auditions are held annually and the award, administered by the Marian Anderson Scholarship Fund, is open to anyone from sixteen to thirty-two years of age. It is not limited to Philadelphia.

Sharing an annual spotlight with the Philadelphia Award on our local scene is the Poor Richard Club's Gold Medal of Achievement, whose recipients cover an even wider field than the former because it is not presented on any local basis. President Dwight D. Eisenhower got one of these medals (when he was a General) and others honored by the club include Walt Disney (who received the first one in 1934), the late Admiral Richard E. Byrd, the *Bulletin's* Robert McLean, Vice President Richard M. Nixon (in 1956), Will Rogers, Bob Hope, industrialist Alfred P. Sloan, Captain Eddie Rickenbacker, David Sarnoff, General Henry H. Arnold, and the nation's defense boss Charles E. Wilson.

The Franklin Medal, bestowed by the Franklin Institute, naturally pays tribute to "workers in physical science or technology . . . whose efforts have done most to advance a knowledge of physical science or its application." It is international in scope, was started in 1914, and was a gift of Chicago's Samuel Insull.

The Gimbel Award is limited to milady. It is presented each year to a woman of the area whose life has been marked by a service to humanity. Winners include Dr. Catharine Macfarlane, Mrs. Efrem Zimbalist, Miss Frances A. Wister, Mrs. George Horace Lorimer, and Dr. Helen C. Bailey.

Thus far, no award has been established for the person drinking the most Philadelphia water.

Oh yes, and Philadelphia also has the oldest newspaperman's club in the country—the Pen and Pencil Club.

It also had the first gossip columnist.

Struthers Burt turned up this dubious gentleman in his wonderfully wise and delightfully engaging book about our town, *Philadelphia: Holy Experiment.*

His by-line, Mr. Burt discovered, was "Palinurus Peeper" or "The Pennsylvania Spy."

"Palinurus Peeper" was in action as early as 1776, when the population of the town was 40,000. He covered everything and picked up many of his hot items in the coffeehouses which, presumably, were as smoke-filled as the night clubs of today.

And . . . and here's where you hold your hats . . .

He claimed that he was a member of the American Philosophical Society.

For more than half a century now, Philadelphia has been plagued by a unique problem—pigeons! These pigeons consider the multitudinous cornices and cracks of City Hall their ancestral home. The town has tried many methods of getting rid of the troublesome birds and all it has gotten for its ingenious efforts has been the bird. The pigeons remain triumphant. Unconcerned by all of the varied efforts to oust them from their municipal perches, the thousands of unsolicited feathered friends have continued to hobnob with city officials, ward leaders and other assorted politicians, spreading germs, making noise and literally messing up the whole City Hall area.

It hasn't been an easy triumph for the birds. Through the years of its losing battle, the town has tried to chase them with red paint, with wild hawks, with sandblasting, with water hoses, with gas, with nets, with wire screens, with sodium silicate, with mercury lighting, with electronic hotfoots, with toy lizards. It even recorded shrieks of anguish to blast at them. But this would, in time, it was felt, be even tougher on the people than the pigeons. At one point a desperate city official advised: "Get them drunk!" This was never tried.

In 1945 the municipal fathers even flightily passed a law making it illegal to feed the pigeons, a gentle hobby many natives had been following for years. The new law didn't net any pigeon, but one human was arrested. He was a seventy-eight-year-old retired clerk, who wept in court as he told the magistrate that he had never been arrested before, his manner attesting to the fact that this might place a large blemish on a good, clean, respectable life. The magistrate wept with him and released the confessed culprit who had been accused of the heinous crime.

Nobody has been arrested for feeding the birds since that emotion-packed day in court. No other device has been developed to force a mass exodus of the birds from the midtown. And the pigeons still flock around City Hall, dropping their messages of disdain on the courtyards and an occasional new hat, as free as birds anywhere.

How's this for long-distance romance, ladies and gentleman? In 1953 a young man named Saha Acquaye came to the Pennsylvania Academy of the Fine Arts for advanced study in painting and sculpture. He was from the African Gold Coast, which is now Ghana, newest independent country in the British Commonwealth of Nations.

That same year a young girl named Nebuwa Nwozo came to Philadelphia to study at the Woman's Medical College. She was from Ibo in the eastern section of Nigeria. Neither had ever known the other. They met when they became members of the

African Student Union in our town. They fell in love. And in February of 1957 they were married.

Mention of this reminds me that Philadelphia is a big town with considerable international flavor. The huge Naval Base, founded in 1801 and housing one of the biggest shipbuilding yards in the world, and the bustling port help to provide that atmosphere with their sailors and their seamen from many lands. A number of musical bars and plain "joints" in the midtown cater almost exclusively to the guys just off ship and ready for a big time on land.

There are no less than fifty-two foreign consuls in the town, including my good friend Nick (Nicholas E.) Meneses, a wonderfully sentimental and warmhearted little gentleman who has represented Cuba in Philadelphia for some twenty-six years.

And there are hundreds of foreign students at the colleges and hospitals in town. Each year the foreign students attending the schools in the metropolitan area produce a Festival of Nations as a gesture of appreciation to International House (at 3905 Spruce Street) and the Philadelphians who have made them welcome in the new land.

Drama, dancing and music characteristic of the students' varied homelands are presented at the colorful affair, which was moved to the country for the first time in 1957 and staged in the barn of prize novelist Pearl S. Buck's farm near Dublin. Acting as hosts with Miss Buck were Mr. and Mrs. James A. Michener and Mr. and Mrs. Oscar Hammerstein II.

Participating in the show were representatives of nine nationalities—African, British, Chinese, French, Italian, Hawaiian, Pakistani, Israeli, and Thai. There was a British monologue, a traditional Scottish dance, French songs with guitar accompaniment, a montage of Italian dancing, interpretative dancing from Pakistan, folk dances from Thailand, a Chinese version of "Little Red Riding Hood," African music and—inevitably—the Hawaiian hula. The show was produced by Robert Huang from Shanghai, China, who studied at the University of Pennsylvania and is now a construction engineer.

Members of the board of trustees of the praiseworthy International House are Mrs. Joseph B. VanderVeer, of Bryn Mawr, the chairman; Mrs. Walter C. Pew, of Bryn Mawr; Mrs. Charles G. Berwind, of Radnor; Philip Klein, of Bryn Mawr; Mrs. Louis E. Levinthal, of Philadelphia; Mrs. Norman D. Palmer, of Berwyn; Mrs. Edwin Wolf II, of Wyncote; Miss Esther H. Leeds, of Germantown; Mrs. Jerome Shestack, of Philadelphia; and Mrs. Samuel Scheidy, of Drexel Hill.

The man who makes money in the strangest way in Philadelphia is a big, handsome, goodhearted guy named Jack Segal. He operates the Fair-Mount Stables.

The basic business of the Fair-Mount Stables is to rent horses for riding. But there is a sideline business, too. The horses make dividends. And Jack Segal makes extra money by selling . . . well, horse manure—and that's no bull.

I once asked Jack how much the horses deposited each week.

"About ten tons," he said.

"And how much do you get for it?" I asked him.

"About eight dollars a ton in the open market," he said.

It's not a bad weekly dividend, considering that it requires not the slightest initiative, enterprise or efficiency on Jack's part.

Chapter XVIII

Some Philadelphia Stories, Short

A FEW years ago Gimbels ran a big advertisement congratulating Wanamaker's on its new men's store. Richard C. Bond, youthful president of Wanamaker's, sent a nice thank you note to Arthur C. Kaufmann, executive head of Gimbels. And a few days later in its advertisement Wanamaker's urged everybody to go to Gimbels to see the Holy Land exhibit of the Philadelphia Council of Churches there. You can't be more gentlemanly business competitors than that.

The most cheated thief in history came from Philadelphia. Mrs. Sylvia Waas, wife of advertising man Les Waas, was checked for allergies and the specialist told her to get a sample of dust from the vacuum cleaner in their home. She and her husband filled a shoe box with dust, went to the doctor's office, and found that he had already closed. So they drove on to Broad Street and Olney Avenue and went into a drugstore there to buy some articles they needed. When they returned to their car, the shoe box was gone.

Every evening in our town a gentleman of some fifty-seven years or so, wearing a luxurious overcoat, a cap and two diamond rings on each hand, walks up to a Market Street newsstand in the midtown and buys a copy of *The Daily Worker*.

A dastardly case of sabotage was uncovered one day in the Curtis Publishing Co. building in Independence Square. Unknown saboteurs infiltrated the coffee-dispensing machines on every floor of the building, which houses the offices of *The Saturday Evening Post, Ladies' Home Journal*, and *Holiday*. And out of the machines came paper cups upon which was printed boldly in two colors: "Read *Time* Magazine"—which is definitely not a Curtis publication. The shocking discovery produced consternation, hurried and frantic calls, and high-level conferences. In quick time, then, the insidious cups were removed from all the machines. The Curtis honor was preserved.

Grace Kelly was married to Prince Rainier in Monaco in April of 1956. For weeks before that, business and civic leader Harry Sylk staged a promotional contest in his Sun Ray Drug Co. stores. The first prize was a fourteen-day trip to Europe and there were thousands of entrants. The winner was picked out of a figurative hat early in April of 1956. It turned out to be Grace Kelly, of 4725 Torresdale Avenue—no relation to the Princess.

One night in October of 1956 Vice President Richard M. Nixon was in town to be greeted by the populace. That, coupled with the fact that the usual Wednesday night shopping crowds were out in full force, had made traffic extremely congested on the midtown streets. Patrick Dennis, author of *Auntie Mame*, the hit play based on his book, was here too, since it was the opening week for that show. He picked up a cab driven by Warren McCauley at Seventh and Walnut streets. "The Warwick," he told the cabbie. "But there's no hurry. I don't have anything to do until the show's over."

The Warwick Hotel is only about ten blocks from Seventh and Walnut but, as both driver and passenger expected, it was a long, slow trip. When they finally arrived, Dennis hopped out of the cab, handed McCauley two dollars, and said: "Thank you for a delightful week end."

A small boy called the Academy of Music box office with an urgent message during an important concert one night.

"I want to speak to Mr. Schwartz," he said.

The man in the box office thought he meant Sam Schwartz, who was once an executive of the Academy.

"Mr. Schwartz isn't here any more," he said.

"Yes, he is," the boy insisted. "He's in the audience. Bernard Schwartz and his wife. They're at the concert."

"Why do you want them?" the boy was asked.

"I'm their son and I don't like the baby-sitter," he said. "I want them to come home."

Before the dinner celebrating Dr. Catharine Macfarlane's seventy-ninth birthday in 1956, the noted cancer specialist went through a session with the newpaper and television cameramen. After they had gotten her to pose this way and that, to look over here and over there, she said wryly: "You know, boys, from any angle I'm no Grace Kelly!"

Back in 1953 Chuck Bednarik, the all-time Penn and Eagles' football great, was doing some television shows in Reading when he wasn't busy with his grid chores. Former Eagles' stars Al Wistert and Bosh Pritchard (who is still an announcer in town), older veterans of "show biz," had been giving the big, easygoing Bednarik pointers, trying to teach him a few tricks in a game that was new and a bit frightening to him. One evening they ran into him at Helen Sigel Wilson's restaurant and asked him how he was coming along.

"I've been doing a little better," he told them. "I feel easier now. I'm even adding a little lib once in a while."

Herman Comer was at the Earle Theater when Warner Bros. opened it in 1924. He was a balcony usher. And he was there when the Warner Bros. ownership came to an end in 1953. He was the manager.

(Comer is now the assistant advertising and publicity boss for the theater company in the town.)

Jimmy O'Connor, a newspaper compositor who lives in Upper Darby, started out of his home one Saturday afternoon to get a Christmas tree. "While you're out," his wife told him, "you might as well get the kid a haircut." So Jimmy and his son left the house and Jimmy yelled back to his wife, "What kind do you want?" Meaning the haircut. "Short and full-blown," she shouted. Meaning the tree.

"Short and full-blown," Jimmy told the barber.

"I never heard of that kind," said the barber.

"Well, that's what the wife *said*," Jimmy explained. "Short and full-blown. I guess she means short all around with lots left on top."

That's the way the son's hair was cut.

When the two of them got home with the tree and the haircut, respectively, Mrs. O'Connor took one look at the boy, gasped, and said: "My goodness, we could stand *him* up in the corner and use him for a tree!"

There is a manufacturing outfit called the King Fifth Wheel Co. on North Second Street in our town. I often heard about those fifth wheels but never knew they really manufactured them.

One day in Room 676, City Hall, attorney Samuel A. Levin had a client who was charged with operating a still. The lawyer asked Judge Herbert E. Millen to continue the case.

The judge asked why.

"My client's on the jury in Room 453," explained the lawyer—and he had the jury list to prove it.

(I wouldn't be paying proper tribute to a deserving citizen if I didn't add a serious word or two here about my friend Sam Levin. Ever since World War II he has had a second career—that of providing parties, entertainment and special affairs of many kinds for the wounded servicemen in the veteran's hospitals in the area. He undertook this work on his own, has devoted hundreds of hours to it, has enlisted the help of numerous City Hall leaders and employees in his program—many of the girls act as hostesses for the vets—and continues it today with the same zeal and enthusiasm that he possessed when he first started.)

Guess Philadelphia just *isn't* as busy as New York.

Movie publicist Milt Young called the home office of Columbia Pictures over there to discuss the opening of *My Sister Eileen* at the Stanley Theater in our town.

A girl answered. He identified himself.

"Young's on the phone," he heard her shout across the office to her boss.

"Couldn't you at least say Milt Young?" he asked her jokingly.

"Well," she told him, "we're awfully pressed for time over here."

Miss Augusta Wagner, associate headmistress of the exclusive Shipley School in Bryn Mawr, has lived a rather full life. She has met and known many important persons and has gotten around quite a bit in her time. Her career as an educator includes service in the Orient (at Yenching University in Peking, China) from 1925 to 1944. One night during a dinner at the school the name of Elvis Presley somehow sneaked into the conversation.

"Who is this Elvis Presley?" asked Miss Wagner. "I never heard of him."

One of the older girls stared at her with an expression compounded of utter disbelief and pity, and said soulfully: "Oh, Miss Wagner, never heard of Elvis Presley? Miss Wagner, you just haven't lived!"

The moderator for a debate between mayoralty candidates Richardson Dilworth (who won) and young advertising man Thacher Longstreth (who lost with the other Republicans) before the Golden Slipper Square Club back in 1955 was Arthur Littleton, former chancellor of the Philadelphia Bar Association. As he was leaving the Bellevue-Stratford Hotel after the battle of words, Littleton was being complimented by everyone on the impartial and efficient manner in which he had handled what could have been an explosive situation.

Among those offering congratulations was attorney Emil F.

Goldhaber, GOP candidate for district attorney in 1957. After Goldhaber had uttered his words of praise, he asked Littleton, "By the way, are you Republican or Democrat?" Littleton smiled and replied: "I would just as soon not say, but I'm going over to the Union League to get my hat and coat."

Gordon Whitcraft, of the *Bulletin* editorial staff, was riding into work on the West Chester local one morning. A moth was fluttering up and down the window next to which he was seated. As the commuting Mr. Whitcraft took out his wallet to get his ticket ready for the conductor, the moth flew into the wallet. When the conductor arrived to punch the ticket, the moth flew out of the wallet. The conductor shook his head, grinned and said: "Well, I've read about it lots of times, but I've never seen it before."

Two little boys were standing along the route of the President Eisenhower parade here in 1955.

"What's the President doing in town?" said one of the boys.

"I don't know for sure," said his pal, "but I think he came here for Del Ennis Night."

"Philadelphia," comic Jack E. Leonard once remarked from the stage of the Latin Casino, "is the city where William Penn has been standing on City Hall for 240 years waiting for Ben Franklin's kite to come back."

Philadelphia cabdrivers are the greatest storytellers in the world. Perhaps this is true of cabbies everywhere. Of that, I can't be sure, but I know it's true in Philly. They are the philosophers of the town.

There was a dark, cold night in November of 1951. Inside the cab it was warm and comfortable, and you were glad to be going home to the soft chair, the good book, the interesting television show.

"The guys over there in Korea," the cabdriver said, "they won't have a lot to be thankful for until they're back home.

"Sure, it's good to be alive," he continued, as you moved on through the now quiet and peaceful park, "but that's something you sort of take for granted. Right?

"Those guys over in Korea are glad they're still alive, sure, but it's what you call a negative sort of thing.

"Over here, sure, we got a lot to be thankful for. We'll be eating our turkey in comfort. I remember when I ate it sitting in the snow in France.

"And we can be glad that they're just practicing with that atom bomb so far. Tests, that's all. We can be glad there ain't any world war yet. Right?"

And, in his fashion, that cabdriver just about summed it up for that long-ago Thanksgiving of 1951, looking at the big picture rather than the private and personal little snapshot. In a way, it had been the year of the dark, cold night.

I remember a happier Christmas story. It is a little Yuletide tale about one Christmas Eve when Santa Claus walked out of the Bellevue-Stratford Hotel and made his rounds in a taxicab.

Now you may not believe that the jolly gentleman from the North Pole ever stopped at a Philadelphia hotel or that he ever rode around our town in a cab. But then, if you are that kind of person, you do not believe that he travels all around the world in a sleigh or slides down a million chimneys in one night, either— and it won't matter. However, if you are one of those who know that Santa is actually a host of good things on a very good day, from the joyful look in a youngster's eyes to the waiting kiss on a grandmother's lips, you will be certain that it was nobody else but Kris Kringle.

A cabdriver told me the story one rainy summer night on the way home and, like most cabbies, he had a way with words. He painted a picture. He had already done some vivid portraits of the various types he had had as fares and then he said, "But I'll tell you the best one I ever had . . .

"It was on a Christmas Eve," he said. "I was just starting out on the job. I pulled in at the Bellevue. I was only there a couple of minutes when this guy comes out of the hotel. He puts a hundred-dollar bill on the wheel."

"Like to be my driver for tonight?" he asked the cabbie.

"I'm your driver," the cabbie told him.

"Fine. Let's go."

"That hundred dollars will cover a lot of travel," the cabbie pointed out.

"We're going to do a lot of traveling," the man said.

The man, as the cabbie explained, was middle-aged and well dressed. He had once lived in Philadelphia, but he hadn't been back to the city for a long time and he was making up for it. He wanted to go around and see all of his old friends, and he was loaded down with packages for them. So they started out and they drove around until it was getting on to ten o'clock.

"It is a practice with me," the cabbie told his fare, "to go home on my lunch hour. Gives me a chance to see the wife and kids and have a snack with them. And I would particularly like to do it tonight. It is always open house at our place on Christmas Eve, sir, and I would deem it a pleasure to have you lunch with us."

"It will be a pleasure," said the man in the cab.

The cabbie's face advertised a happy memory, as he painted another scene on this rainy summer evening.

"Well," he said, "you could tell this gentleman was accustomed to nothing but the best. But he joined our little family group and he sat there at the table just as though he had spent all his life in little houses like mine.

"The wife thought he was the nicest man she's ever met, and he made her feel mighty good with all of his well-chosen compliments about her food.

"And when we left he insisted that she take a twenty-dollar bill, and he slipped tens to each of my three youngsters."

The two of them, the cabbie and his fare, returned then to their work and they drove around delivering the packages until about three o'clock in the morning. And finally all of the stops had been made, all of the old friends seen, all of the gifts delivered.

"I guess that does it," the man told the cabbie. "And here's a little gift for all of your help."

The "little gift" made the cabbie $100 richer, and he turned to say thanks and the man said, "You've been fine company."

And then quickly the man hopped out of the cab and hustled back into the hotel.

"Well, I hurried home to help trim the tree," the cabbie said, "and I just walked in the house like nothing had happened. I went up to the wife and I said to her, 'Here's a hundred dollars for you, honey.' Just like that, casual.

"It was something, I'm telling you. Can you imagine something like that happening? You start out on a night's work and it turns out so good you feel like crying . . ."

Sure, the gentleman had a name, the cabbie said. This had happened some years ago. And the cabbie had forgotten it or he didn't think it was proper to tell it or, maybe, as the cabbie said, maybe it really didn't matter.

"He could have had only one name," the cabbie said. "I was a dope not to recognize him the minute he walked out of the hotel. Even those kids of mine know Santa Claus when they see him."

I haven't told the story of the Lloyds, which is one that many people in the town knew and talked about. Nicholas P. Lloyd, Jr., a onetime Philadelphia business executive who had once been a big spender in the night clubs, finally had to file a petition for bankruptcy in the U.S. District Court. His liabilities, the newspaper stories said, were listed at $651,911. His assets, they said, were approximately $250 in goods and cash. And, give a dollar here and there, that was just about the size of it. When Nick Lloyd had it, he spent it good. And when he didn't have it, he still spent it. And that was just about the story of Nick Lloyd and his money.

An attractive and buxom blonde named Peggy Lloyd came to town for the first time back in 1951 and created something of a sensation at a spot called the Zodiac Room, then operated by Jack Lynch and now gone from the midtown scene. To start with, she had a stunning figure in the Jane Russell style—and she wore the kind of gowns to emphasize it. And thus bountifully equipped for popularity even before she sang her first note, she strolled from table to table with a hand mike to give her tunes the intimate touch for the patrons.

Among the men who went to take a look and listen was a familiar face in the gay spots, a big spender named Nick Lloyd. He went, he saw, and he was conquered. In time they were married and she quit working and retired from the singing business. And almost everybody said that it wouldn't last, that they'd just have a fling at good times together for a while and then it would fade away like the old generals. And let's not kid ourselves, they lived it up real good. Peggy had furs and Peggy had jewels. They dined in style wherever they went, with the champagne bucket an inevitable part of the table tableau. They had big parties in their big hotel apartment. They had many guests. And Nick was always buying for friends who stopped at their table when they dined. He was always buying drinks and grabbing tabs and tipping big. Until the money ran out.

When Nick went broke *everybody* was sure that it wouldn't last. A lot of bets could have been lost on that one. Peggy went back to the singing business to pay off some bills. Peggy stuck with Nick. The jewels went, the trinkets went. She had only her wedding ring the first night of her "return" engagement.

"This is all that's left," she told me.

"Last year this time," she said, and she was smiling about it, "last year this time I had a laundress, a cleaning woman, a housekeeper, and a masseuse to slap me around.

"Now," she said, "I got me. And a vacuum cleaner and a scrub brush. But you know something, my advice to anyone and everyone is to go broke once in your life. You learn a lot. You learn a heck of a lot."

A well-constructed girl from a ramshackle, weather-beaten old farmhouse in a desolate strip of land some forty miles from Logan, West Virginia, came to town to perform in the musical bars featuring the girlie shows. She was an exotic dancer and made enough money out of stripping for a living to buy a big roomy house on the hillside for her family.

Two weeks after she came to town, the house back home burned down. The stage name of the exotic dancer was—and is—Blaze Starr and the tag line that goes with it is "Miss Spontaneous Combustion."

And lawdy knows I can't forget the most eccentric and bizarre piano player who ever came to town. That—and it's not even a contest—would be Forrest Sykes, a real gone guy from Kansas City who has spent his life making high-class jazz music in low-class dives.

Forrest had some long stays in town. At times it seemed that he might become a permanent fixture. But that wasn't his way. A fellow with an infinite capacity for both rhythm and gin, Forrest, after thrilling the customers at numerous clubs with his wild and exciting keyboard pyrotechnics, just strolled out of town one night and left no announcement behind. Nobody heard from him and reports drifted back that he had died in every kind of setting from bistro to telephone booth.

Then, about a year later, he just strolled back into town, as though he had never been away.

"I been kinda ill," he explained, "but I ain't daid yet.

"I been between Kansas City and Chicago," he said. "I lost all my family except my daughter. Georgia died. And there was nothing else to stay around the West for. I'm gonna make me some money and buy me a limousine and buy me a home here. I just been driftin'. Now I'm gonna get me some new white tails and settle down."

Forrest always appeared for work in tails—when he had the money for them. He strode majestically into the spot where he was working. He never merely announced the name of his next number, but would present "my conception of 'Glow Worm'" or "my rendition of 'Big Fat Mama.'" And he played with feverish intensity, imagination and humor. He was no major artist, no outstanding character, but when he sat down at his piano, lifted his tails behind the bench, peered proudly over the audiences in his smoke-foggy rooms, and played, he was a king—uncrowned, unsung, unknown, but a king in his own private and special domain.

When he wasn't at the piano, he was just a guy who never had any money or any future. He mixed up his nights and days, and guzzled like there was no tomorrow. He played his first honky-tonk when he was fifteen. He is now about thirty-one and he has lived maybe 231 years with his nights.

"Lawdy, I have had a fabulous time," he said once. "My mama

always told me: 'You keep on goin' and you gonna be lucky you be around at thirty.' One never knows, do one?"

I don't know whether Forrest's mama was right or not. Nobody in town has heard anything from Forrest for a couple of years now and reports have drifted back that he has died in every kind of setting from bistro to telephone booth. So he's about due to stroll back into town again, just as though he had never been away.

Chapter XIX

The Local Diet Includes Birdseed

THEY must feed the kids birdseed in Philly.

It is not only the home of scrapple, pepper pot, ice cream and the cinnamon bun. It is also, to a degree no other city even closely approaches, the home of the nation's most popular—and frequently its best—singers.

And it all started long before my time in the town. An old-timer named Thomas H. Keenan, a former Kensington resident who had moved to Ocean City, New Jersey, once briefed me on the earlier days.

"First," he said, "there was the late Charlie Boyden, who was with the Dumont and Emmet Welch minstrels. Al Jolson got a lot of his style from him.

"And when records from Victor [the big RCA Victor plant, incidentally, is right across the river in that good-neighbor city, Camden] were seventy-five cents in the early days of victrolas, Jim McCool's cost a dollar. He was the acknowledged baritone of his day, and his day was from about 1910 to 1920.

"Vaughan Comfort had the lead singing role in several Ziegfeld *Follies*. Both of these men were from Kensington.

"Charlie Dooin was a nationally known tenor. He managed the Phillies once, too. Jack Norworth, who wrote 'Take Me Out to the Ball Game,' was a great singer of popular songs and nationally known, too. And did you know that Preston Foster was a fine singer with La Scala of South Philadelphia and went to Hollywood on contract as such? But gangsters and detectives became popular in the movies at that time and Preston looked the part of both.

"There were also Rae Dooley, who married Eddie Dowling, and her brother Jimmy from West Philadelphia, who were musical comedy stars of the very first rank. So was Frank Tinney, of South Philly, and so was Elizabeth Murray, of St. Edward's parish at Germantown Avenue and York. She was a big-time musical comedy star and a great singer in vaudeville.

"If there had been talking pictures, jukeboxes, radio and TV in their day, they all would have been names that became household words. Charlotte Greenwood was a great comedy singer and she came out of Philly, too. So did Julia Sanderson, one of the best . . ."

And perhaps it all began in a more modern day with an amiable fellow named Frankie Richardson, who is virtually forgotten now about the country but still shouts his old tunes in the night clubs in his home town. Hairline receding, the years running ads in his face, he has played them all and, in recent years, they have usually been the second-rate spots. But his manner is as jaunty as ever when he trots on to the floor with his walking stick and sings something like "Everywhere You Go," which he introduced way back in 1926.

Frankie, who gained his experience in the Dumont and Welch minstrel troupes, was the Sinatra-Como-Crosby-Presley of his day. His national reputation dimmed years ago but once he was a big star, the singing idol of the first talking musicals produced in Hollywood, introducing to the nation numbers like "Walking with Susie" and "I'm in the Market for You" in such pioneer sound movies as the Fox Movietone *Follies* and *Sunny Side Up*. Frankie's place in the film firmament faded quickly and his glory days were soon gone. But apparently he set a pattern that has made our big town a veritable factory of vocal talent, turning out human songbirds with almost assembly line efficiency.

No other city—not even New York—has come close to producing such a large number of singers who have perched high on the old ladder of success in the entertainment world, their voices soaring through theaters and auditoriums, riding the busy air waves, bursting forth from the gaudy jukeboxes and spinning endlessly on the record players. It is no sudden state of affairs but the situation has become so pronounced within recent years—principally because of the impact of records on the music business—that any outsider must harbor the notion that parents *do* feed birdseed to their kids in Philly.

Consider some pertinent facts:

It wasn't too many years after the eclipse of Frankie Richardson that a onetime newspaperman (the *Bulletin*) and choir soloist (the Grace Baptist Temple, Dr. Conwell's church) named Nelson Eddy and a pretty thing named Jeannette MacDonald (West Philly High), finding their way to Hollywood on separate roads, joined vocal forces and became a romantic singing team that was movie box-office magic for a long time.

Not too long after they had wandered off the screens, another Philadelphian with an even bigger voice than Eddy's came along to thrill a nation of filmgoers and record buyers. This, of course, was Mario Lanza, a man whose vast temperament is exceeded only by the vastness of his dimensions from time to time. His girth and his eccentricities have played havoc with what could have been a tremendously notable career, but his records are still, invariably, big sellers.

There was, too, in the young days of radio, that extremely popular Arthur Tracy, The Street Singer, to match fans with Bing Crosby and Russ Columbo. In the pop music field, in this day when records provide an unprecedented amount of fame, cash and the impetus that leads to success in other show business media, the Quaker City performers have been having an amazingly rewarding time for themselves.

Young Eddie Fisher joined the elite of the male pop singers in 1954 when his discs outsold those of Crosby, Perry Como, Frankie Laine and the other old-time masters and long-time favorites, setting the stage for his own television show and top stardom. Early in 1957, Eddie made his first appearance at a local night club since 1948 when he arrived at the Latin Casino. In 1948 he had played this same spot, but then he was an unknown, singing the production numbers with the chorus girls. Now he was a big star and it made for a strange night in a club.

This is the way I began my column on Eddie's return to the home town, on his opening at the club:

SOCIAL NOTES FROM ALL OVER: Mr. Eddie Fisher, a former resident, is visiting in Philadelphia. On Friday night he entertained his parents and a host of friends at a most enjoyable party in the Latin Casino. A good time was had by all.

Mr. Fisher now resides in Hollywood with his wife, Debbie, and their little daughter, Carrie. He is engaged in the entertainment business and has been quite successful, having won many honors in his particular field. All of his local friends wish him well.

It was that kind of night. That was the feeling you had as you watched Eddie's opening show. He had made good in the big world, and there was a small-town atmosphere in the packed room. It was an unusual crowd, too, for a club, a crowd of all ages and numerous family groups. There were old folks and small fry, middle-aged people and teen-aged girls. And they were from all classes. The Kiwanians and their families in Ford City, Pennsylvania, might have been honoring a local boy who had just been appointed assistant cashier of a big bank in Pittsburgh, Pennsylvania. That was the way it seemed that night in our big town.

While Fisher was pushing his way past the long-time jukebox kings in the male fraternity that year, a pert, cute girl named Kitty Kallen was dislodging Patti Page and Joni James from their throne on the distaff side. Miss Kallen, who had grown up in the same South Philly neighborhood as Fisher and Lanza, went on to stage musicals and Hollywood movies.

And from that same section of row houses along poor streets have come many other young men and women to brighten a nation's hours with their music. That list would include Buddy Greco, Al Martino, Mary Ann McCall, Sunny Gale, Frankie Lester, Jimmy Saunders, Micki Marlo, Joe Valino, Georgie Shaw,

Cathy Allen, Gloria Mann, Vince Carson, Rita Konstance, Dick Merrick and, most recently, Eddie Dano and Charlie Gracie.

Most of them were formerly vocalists with the most popular bands, when bands were in their heyday. Greco was with Goodman, Miss McCall with Charlie Barnett, Saunders with Harry James, Carson with Jimmy Dorsey, Miss Allen with Louis Prima, Lester with Buddy Morrow and Merrick with Jerry Wald.

And many other Philadelphia singers, from other sections, have become well known from hit records, television appearances or band vocalizing. These would include Dick Lee, who became a regular performer on Sid Caesar's television show; Bob Manning, the lanky fellow many in the music business think is as good as any; Pat Kirby, a regular on Steve Allen's old "Tonight" show (as was Miss Marlo); network radio songstress Sandy Stewart; and Dolores O'Neill, now retired, and Hilde Simmons, still busy, both of whom were at one time the larks with Gene Krupa's band; Jackie Lee, also a performer at the piano; and society lark Anne Francine, who is popular in Paris and America's supper clubs.

As if that weren't enough, one of the steady best-selling groups on wax is the Four Aces, led by Al Alberts, who studied journalism at Temple University. They make a mighty comfortable living with their harmonizing. And the undisputed international rajahs of rock 'n' roll music are Bill Haley and his Comets from out Chester way, who have prompted demonstrations wherever they have gone, including Australia and Great Britain. Featured in many of the tumult-producing rock 'n' roll movies have been Freddie Bell and the Bellboys and Dave Appel and the Applejacks.

All of these names are only a beginning, a part of the list of Quaker City singers who have earned happy headlines, heavy cash and hearty applause. First and foremost and most distinguished on any Philadelphia list is the internationally famous Marian Anderson, who possesses one of the most acclaimed voices of our time and who became the first Negro ever to sing with the Metropolitan Opera Company.

Two other Negro favorites who have been among the great entertainers of our day and who began their careers on the same home grounds are Ethel Waters, with her sad and memorable blues voice; and the inimitable Pearl Bailey, with her "Tired" and cynical one. Incidentally, Miss Waters, who hails from Chester, was billed as "Sweet Mama Stringbean" in her first local appearance.

A younger girl, Bertice Redding, from West Philly, although almost completely unknown in her home town, has been a London favorite for the last couple of years.

Although better known for their comedy, both Imogene Coca and Ronny Graham have sung in Broadway stage hits; and to the musical comedy stage the town has also contributed the veterans of so many shows, Vivienne Segal, Larry Douglas, Mark Dawson, Wilbur Evans and Eddie Roecker.

In the operatic and concert fields, aside from Miss Anderson, the list is an imposing one that would include Margaret Harshaw, the principal Wagnerian soprano at the Met now; David Poleri, who has made headlines in the Lanza fashion; Virginia MacWatters, Frank Guarrera, Brenda Lewis, Lois Hunt, Anna Moffo (from Wayne), Dolores Wilson, Helena Scott, Tom Perkins, Lillian Shelby, Elizabeth Doubleday, and Walter Fredericks (from Camden, which is not only the home of RCA Victor but of Campbell's soups).

Another tag line is in order for Philadelphia, it would seem. They can start to call it the City of Singers, too. And the singers are only the beginning. Only the beginning, ladeez and gentulmen!

Let us now take up Philadelphia and some other arts, both major and minor. Because, for a city that is supposed to be a sleepy one, not given overly much to bright lights and gay times, Philadelphia has made an amazing contribution to the entertainment world, to what Gilbert Seldes called the lively arts, to popular music, to classical music, to art itself and to sundry other vital aspects of American life like . . . well, say, baseball.

It would be difficult for any town to lead off a local parade of vocal talent with a more illustrious pair than Marian Anderson and Mario Lanza, of course. But that's only the singing business. In the theater our town starts with Edwin Forrest, the Drews, the Davenports and the Barrymores, which isn't a bad starting point at all.

For the comedy that brings much-needed laughter to the people, it can start with a similarly esteemed figure, that of the late, bulbous-nosed, billiard-playing, booze-imbibing, inimitably funny W. C. Fields, who first learned the less dubious art of thievery as a vagabond boy in the streets of Philadelphia.

Fields can be followed by Ed Wynn, now making an impressive comeback as a straight dramatic actor. And then consider the list that can be made of actors of varied types in the movies and on the stage, starting with the old-timers: Janet Gaynor, Phil Baker, Florence Reed, Walter Kelly (*The Virginia Judge*, of that famous Kelly clan), Nelson Eddy, Jeannette MacDonald, Helen Broderick, Penny Singleton, Jack Whiting, Ethel Waters, Preston Foster (from just across the river on Jersey soil), Arthur Tracy, El Brendel, Vivienne Segal, Charlotte Greenwood, George Bancroft and Eddie Quillan.

Skip to the moderns and you turn up with: Imogene Coca and Nancy Walker (just about the two top American comediennes of our day), Grace Kelly (the princess who was the nearest thing to an American queen for a number of years—and from that same Kelly family, naturally), Paul Douglas (once a radio announcer in the town), Cass Dailey, Broderick Crawford, Joan McCracken, Eddie Fisher, Keenan Wynn (Ed's funny son), Pearl Bailey (who grew up and learned her trade here), actor-director Ezra Stone, Ronny Graham (whose father Steve is still a booking agent in the town), young Broadway and television actors Martin Gabel, Mark Richman, Keith Andes, Staats Cotsworth, John Connell, and Patricia Jenkins, new screen actor James Darren (formerly Ercolani), wrestler turned actor Mike Lane (who made such an impressive hit in the picture *The Harder They Fall*), stage and movie actor Rudy Bond (once a newsboy on Market Street), movie actors Lyle Bettger and Malcolm Atterbury, stage actor Iggie Wolfington, and film starlets Linda March (Sussman), Marian (Sue) Randall, who has also acted on Broadway, Dolores Donlon (formerly Pat Vaniver), Jeanne Ferguson (like Pat, a former model about town), and Rebecca Welles.

You can add one of the best stage directors of the day, Morton DaCosta, who went through his theater apprenticeship with the Templayers of Temple University; and veteran movie producer

Joseph Pasternak, who was responsible for introducing Deanna Durbin to the screen.

For playwrights, you start with one of the pioneers in stage realism, George Kelly (that family's in again!), and then among the moderns you have Clifford Odets, the exciting voice of the Thirties; John Cecil Holm, with his flair for comedy; Joseph Kramm, who authored the Pulitzer Prize-winning *The Shrike*; Albert Hackett; and, most recently, N. Richard Nash and Harry Kurnitz.

These are some of the best-known figures, the major league array. But the minor leagues are active, too. I doubt that any other city has so many active and frequently excellent little theater groups. *Stalag 17*, later a big hit on both stage and screen, was first presented in a nonprofessional production by one of those busy little outfits, the Plays and Players. And Jasper Deeter and his Hedgerow Theater are nationally famous for their contributions to the stage from a place in the country.

Aside from its playwrights, Philadelphia has an impressive array of other writers in all fields to offer to the literary world from its city proper and the suburbs which have always been considered an integral—and important—part of the town.

And at this point it should be mentioned that our town is also the home of the Curtis Publishing Co. and those national family institutions, *The Saturday Evening Post* and the *Ladies' Home Journal* as well as the younger *Holiday*; and of the world-famous Athenaeum of Philadelphia, which was founded in 1814 and has some 100,000 volumes on its library shelves, many of them dealing with the town's history and its notables.

Now, among the writers there is that gracious and charming woman who writes such scholarly and magnificent history, Catherine Drinker Bowen, whose Quaker family is one of the *really* old ones. Struthers Burt has pointed out that the first white child born on the site of Philadelphia was Edward Drinker, whose entrance into the world was made in a log cabin near what is now the intersection of Second and Walnut streets.

There is, along with the highly esteemed lady, the younger Davis Grubb, who turned out one of the most poetic novels of our times in *The Night of the Hunter*.

There is the brilliant and versatile Judge Curtis Bok, who can deal as handily with words as he can with thoughts. He wrote some of his most eloquent words in a 1949 legal decision clearing a group of books of an obscenity charge. Answering the usual arguments of the usual censorship brigade, he wrote some words which are well worth remembering.

"It will be asked," he said, "whether one would care to have one's young daughter read these books. I should prefer that my own three daughters meet the facts of life and the literature of the world in my library, rather than behind a neighbor's barn, for I can face the adversary there directly . . .

"Our daughters must live in the world and decide what sort of women they are to be, and we should be willing to prefer their deliberate and informed choice of decency rather than an innocence that continues to spring from ignorance."

I have the comfortable feeling that many good and true things are safe so long as Judge Bok is around.

There are in the writing ranks, along with Judge Bok, that master of novels touched with artistry, Wright Morris, of Wayne, winner of the 1957 National Book Award; perceptive Main Line novelist Livingston Biddle, Jr.; McCready Huston, public relations man for the Academy of Natural Sciences, who has made the Main Line his province; always engaging Jerre Mangione; Leon (*Battle Cry*) Uris; historical novelists David Livingston and Elizabeth Gray Vining; Richard Powell, the mystery novelist who turned more serious and wrote that best-selling novel about his home town, *The Philadelphian*; Albert Idell, who has pictured the old Philadelphia scene in his novels; and the versatile Hannah Lees.

There are mystery novelists Bart Spicer, who has also penned a couple of historical volumes; William McGivern, Joseph Shallit and Samuel Krasney; Negro novelist William Gardner Smith, now living in Paris; skilled novelist Seymour Shubin; Western novelist C. Hall Thompson; humorist Caskie Stinnett; action novelist-screen writer David Goodis; novelists Walt Sheldon and James S. Montgomery, editor-critic-Penn professor Charles Lee; and Hollis Alpert, the movie critic of *The Saturday Review*.

And up in Bucks County there are scores of men and women busy at their typewriters in a rustic setting, headed by that prolific and famous author of *Tales of the South Pacific*, James A. Michener. My friend Jim is not at home much any more. Too busy traveling about the world, knocking out dramatic and significant books like *The Bridge at Andau* in a hurry.

To give you some indication of the millions of printed words which were born in the obviously inspirational Bucks County atmosphere, consider this: Early in 1957 Kenyon Nicholson, proprietor of the Delaware Book Shop in New Hope, made a window display featuring books by authors who had lived and worked in that area. He counted 120 of them. Not 120 books. A hundred and twenty authors.

They ranged from John Greenleaf Whittier, who worked a spell in Upper Solebury, to Michener, Pearl Buck and Budd Schulberg of the present. And they included Dorothy Parker, S. J. Perelman, Glenway Westcott, Nathanael West, Millen Brand, James Gould Cozzens, Paul Gallico, Moss Hart, Oscar Hammerstein, Katherine Anne Porter, Sam and Bella Spewack, Allen Tate, George S. Kaufman, Martha Albrand, Ruth and Augustus Goetz, and Paul Bowes. Not to mention Kenyon Nicholson himself—and Artie Shaw.

It's quite a territory for folks who deal in putting words together nicely, this Philadelphia territory. The late Christopher Morley, of Haverford, and his fictional daughter, Kitty Foyle, of Kensington, would be mighty proud of their home town on the that score.

Of all the Philadelphia writers, there is no doubt that the most colorful is my friend Dave Grubb, both a brooding and a witty gentleman, who likes the late hours and loves to observe the actions of the Night People, talk to the strange types and add to his storehouse of knowledge about the way *all* people live and think and act.

He has been a familiar member of the Night People fraternity himself and he sometimes wears rather eccentric garb. For a time he donned the kind of outfit worn by his idol, Sean O'Casey, in a sort of personal tribute to that literary giant and as a challenge to the world which he felt had failed to give proper appreciation to O'Casey's creative work.

It was while dressed thusly that he was arrested one night. He was at one of his favorite haunts, Jack Dubin's Hi-Fi Room in the old Rittenhouse Hotel—a popular gathering place for a surprisingly varied clientele, including those who follow the arts and those who are engaged in them. He had been drinking and was charged, for no good and sufficient reason, with intoxication.

Now, just as there is no doubt that Dave has his eccentricities, so there is no doubt that magistrates—the minor judiciary in our town—are hardly intellectual giants. There are some goodhearted, fair and genial men among them, to be sure. There couldn't be a nicer gentleman or a better guy than Magistrate Samuel Clark, Jr., for instance. Everybody likes Sammy. But to most of them a scribbler of words would not be a leading citizen. And to none of them would Davis Grubb appear to be a successful author.

The morning after the raid on the Hi-Fi Room—the police action in this case was ridiculous and smacked more of Gestapo than justice—Dave was brought before the magistrate, a real old-timer in the ranks of the minor judiciary. He took a look at Dave, who was wearing a crumpled gray sports coat with a cap to match, was smiling nervously, and was evidencing the strain of the hours in a police cell.

"What kind of a place is this?" he asked, meaning the Hi-Fi Room.

Then he went on to Dave, who was identified by Assistant District Attorney Stanley Bashman as the author of *The Night of the Hunter*.

"Looks like a janitor to me," remarked the judge, in the traditional flip magisterial tone.

Then he discharged him with some advice.

"Go out and get yourself a job," he advised.

Dave didn't bother to tell him that *The Night of the Hunter* had sold to the movies for $75,000.

Chapter XX

The Man's Still Boasting

PHILADELPHIA has a noble tradition in the world of art. There the beginning is with Benjamin West, the first American artist to win distinction on two continents, Gilbert Stuart and Charles Willson Peale.

And the significance is with those daring pioneers, the bitterly condemned graduates of "The Ash Can School"—Thomas Eakins, Robert Henri, and his students, the newspaper illustrators John Sloan, George Luks and William Glackens. They felt that all technique was not enough. They believed in reflecting life in their work. And their careers followed a usual pattern in the arts. The ridicule turned to recognition and that, in time, was followed by reputation, as they gave to American art new vigor, new honesty and new achievement.

Eakins, incidentally, painted one of the most famous fight pictures in the world, the one now hanging in the Museum of Art on the Parkway. The scene is the old Arena at Broad and Cherry streets and all of the main figures in the painting—completed here in 1899—were from the town. They are fighter Billy Smith; Billy McCarney and Elwood (the Old War Horse) McCloskey, who are in his corner; and Clarence Cranmer, the timer, who was a newspaper friend of the artist.

Good and able hands have picked up the paints and the brushes left behind by these men. Their work is being carried on creatively and excitingly by a host of artists busy at their easels in the Greater Philadelphia area. Of the forty-one artists invited to show their work at an annual exhibition in the Pennsylvania Academy of the Fine Arts (co-sponsor: the Philadelphia Water Color Club) early in 1957, fifteen were from the metropolitan area. They were Alfred Bendiner, Morris Blackburn, Jack Bookbinder, Albert Gold (one of my own special favorites), Oliver Grimley, Martin Jackson, John Lear, John McCoy, James Kirk Merrick, Hobson Pittman, Henry C. Pitz, Helen Siegel, Benton Spruance, Walter Stuempfig and Andrew Wyeth (probably the one with the greatest reputation).

Other painters on the local scene include Julius Bloch, Ben Wolf, Abraham P. Hankins, Emlen Etting, Fritz Janschka, Franklin C. Watkins, Francis J. Barone, Robert D. Goldman, Oliver Nuse, Karl Sherman, George Harding, Edward Shenton, Ben Solowey, Humbert L. Howard, Leonard L. Nelson, Raymond G. Hendler, Martin Zipin and Clayton Whitehill. And I could not fail to mention two who died recently, Walter Baum (another of my special favorites and a wonderful old gentleman) and Miss Harriet Sartain, retired dean of the Moore Institute of Art. Her family had played an important part in the growth of graphic arts in the town and her grandfather, John Sartain, introduced the art of mezzotint engraving in the United States.

Outstanding sculptors in the town would include Joseph J. Greenberg, Jr., Raphael Sabatini, Harry Rosin, Rudolph Staffel and Henry Mitchell.

Not a bad aggregation of artists at all—for one town.

And, going from the fairly sublime to the frantically rhythmic, Philadelphia has long been in the forefront in sending young men out over the nation to make hot licks, sweet notes and the solid beat. A couple of Italian boys from South Philly got that trend underway. Eddie Lang, who was Salvatore Massaro as a lad, was the first guitarist to become famous as a jazz soloist on that instrument; and the irrepressible Joe Venuti, a pal of Eddie's who is still around making fun and frolic, was the first white jazz violinist.

Others in the jazz ranks include Lucky Roberts, who was one of the best of the ragtime pianists, trumpeter-leader Charlie Gaines, who played the local spots for years; cornet great Rex Stewart; pianist-leader Charlie Johnson; trumpeter Ziggy Elman, a native who moved to Atlantic City when he was four; and Billy Kyle, that great and not sufficiently praised pianist with Louis Armstrong and his All-Stars.

But it was with bebop, bop, progressive, modern, cool—the newer jazz music of discord and dissonance—that the town really went to the head of the parade. In that milieu the list includes Stan Getz and Charlie Ventura, who have been at the top of the tenor sax list in the music magazine polls for years; Gerry Mulligan, a big man on the baritone sax; Buddy DeFranco, the first to play the modern stuff on the clarinet; Bill Harris, who created a new trombone style; drummer Stan Levey; and Dizzy Gillespie, who, although not a native, developed his new bop trumpet style while playing here for a long period.

And you can't forget, among the musicians of varying styles, that solid girl pianist Beryl Booker, organist Bill Doggett, pianist Buddy Greco, tenor sax man Richie Kamuca, pianist-maestro-arranger Elliot Lawrence, pianist Jimmy Lyon and pianist-composer Bobby Troup.

Nor can you forget—most emphatically not—all of those veterans of the Philadelphia Orchestra, whose names are less known to the general public but who are masters on every instrument; and young concert artists like violinist Norman Carol.

And there is the well-known society maestro Meyer Davis and old-time band leader, Ted Weems, who gave Perry Como his start. And I shudder to think of the ones who have slipped my mind. Almost forgot to put down Billy Krechmer, a guy I know better than any of them.

Billy Krechmer got tired of traveling around and he opened his own place for playing the music he likes. He's a small guy with a receding hairline and a clarinet, and his spot is about as narrow as an old alley in the town and it's on an old street, street called Ranstead, and it's just "a little place where old friends meet." This is where Billy has wound up, happily, playing his kind of music—flitting between the nimble, the moody, the bluesy—after more than thirty years in the business.

"I come from Millville, New Jersey," he told me one night when I was having some memories on the house, "and I began playing in 1925. Playing with a guy by the name of Mickey Guy. We were playing a ballroom on the second floor of a place in an Illinois amusement park.

"And I remember, as you reached the top of the stairs, there was a great big sign:

NO CHARLESTON DANCING

"It was only on girders, this ballroom, and the Charleston and jazz were just beginning. And I guess they were afraid the place might collapse with that new dance. Before, they had played the waltz and then the two-step, which was a slow one. And then the one-step came along. That was where they knocked themselves out.

"Probably nobody remembers it now but I remember going down to Atlantic City to hear Ray Miller's band because Frankie Trumbauer was in it. Everybody was talking about him, about the way he played sax. Seems funny now, but that was the only way you could hear them in those days. There were no records of any worth. There was no radio. No TV. That was the way you had to hear a band in those days—in person.

"Well, the banjo player in those days, he played ragtime. And everybody would say, 'It's a bear.'

"When a guy played good in those days, they said 'He's unconscious.' "

In 1928 Billy was with the Gene Goldkette band (later to become famous as the Casa Loma Orchestra led by Glen Gray) and Joe Venuti, that fiddler from South Philly, was leading it. And Bix Beiderbecke, the legendary cornet man, would come in after hours and blow the gloom right into the sky. And here are some more names for good old Nostalgia U: In 1931 the young man from Millville went with Red Nichols and the Five Pennies, joining such luminaries as Gene Krupa, Joe Sullivan and the late Glenn Miller.

One time, he remembered, they had a deal. Played till ten-thirty intermission at this spot. "And if the crowd wasn't good, you didn't get paid. And if you didn't keep on playing, you got beat up."

Jazz, of course, was not accepted in those days. "And if you played what they called Dixieland at the better places," Billy recalled, "the people chased you. Sweet bands were getting strong, Guy Lombardo, Rudy Vallee and the others.

"I came back here then and I went into the Mastbaum Theater. There were eighty men in the pit band then. Those were the days of the presentation thing. Dick Powell came in, I remember. He had just made his first movie, *Blessed Event*. He was a crooner then and not a private eye. He sang a song called "Crazy People," which went over real big."

Billy opened his Jam Session, his little place on Ranstead Street —which isn't much more than an alley itself—in 1938, mainly, he thought, as a stop for visiting musicians. They liked to get together in impromptu jam sessions then. The musicians' union now bars it.

"That was when the big band business was coming into its own for the first time," he said, "and the kids were jumping in the aisles. The jitterbugs were here. And you could see the enthusiasm growing. Those were the great days for the musicians. They were kings then, and there hasn't been a day like it since."

What killed it? Well, there was a war, the big war. And there was bop.

"After the frantic war era," he said, "people wanted a different kind of music. They wanted to relax with the music, maybe. And bop came along. Too much bop played by too many bad people. Bad people meaning poor musicians. It's an involved type of music and too many who have tried it can't play their instruments.

"But these aren't happy days. Maybe that kind of music goes with them, I don't know. But bop is so unhappy. It's a come-down."

Billy's place turned out to be popular with more than musicians shortly after it was opened, and the changing styles haven't af-

Elfreth's Alley

fected his music at all. With his little outfit of regulars—the instrumentalists stay for long periods in his spot—he has continued to play the old styles. Sometimes the blues, sometimes Dixieland, sometimes nimble, running music that reminds you of the old Benny Goodman Trio or John Kirby's little band from that exciting Era of Swing . . . music that is rambling and rhythmic and subdued and inventive and wild and uninhibited, for relaxing of a night.

"There is no such thing as bad notes," Billy always says. "It's only the way they're played."

The way he plays them, they come out real good.

The town, I confess, hasn't provided the country with too many topflight comedians since it sent W. C. Fields and Ed Wynn out into the world with their striking and singular styles for making laughter. But, in more recent years, it has contributed Imogene Coca to the stage and television arenas and Nancy Walker to the theater scene. Why television hasn't made use of Miss Walker's wonderful knockabout talents is a mystery to me.

And, more recently than that, there have been wry, casual and poker-faced Joey Bishop, with his fresh quips and smart gags, and Pepper Davis and Tony Reese, with their spirited antics. Both of these acts are popular in all of the big night clubs and are frequent guests on the top television shows. Ronny Graham, who made his Broadway debut in a *New Faces* revue, has a big following among the more sophisticated clubgoers with his Freudian routines and savage parodies.

And if the town is a mite neglectful in making laughs for the people, it more than atones for it in the music it makes for them, in creating the tunes they hear, the tunes they hum, the tunes they sing, the tunes they remember. For, in the Philadelphia area, "Nearly Everybody Reads the *Bulletin*"—and almost everybody must write songs.

Among the classical, semiclassical, or serious composers, there are George Antheil, who hails from Trenton but got his start studying and working here; Samuel Barber, born in West Chester and long a leading figure in the modern scene; Marc Blitzstein, who penned "The Cradle Will Rock"; Gian Carlo-Menotti, famed composer of operas like *The Consul* and *The Medium*, who studied at the town's famous Curtis Institute; Dr. Frank Black, late conductor of the NBC Orchestra; Louis Gesensway, veteran member of the Philadelphia Orchestra; Efrem Zimbalist, director of the Curtis Institute, and James Francis Cooke, longtime editor of the recently expired *Etude* magazine, with their standard compositions; and Paul Creston, who teaches at Swarthmore College.

Moose Charlap wrote the score for Mary Martin's big hit *Peter Pan*, and movie scores and background music are being produced regularly by a number of Philadelphians. Perhaps the best known of these men is David Raksin, from Wynnefield, whose big one on the Hit Parade was "Laura." Film score credits for Herman Stein, a Northeast High School graduate, include José Ferrer's *The Great Man*. Alex North, a Chester composer, did the music for the screen version of *A Streetcar Named Desire*. Josef Myrow, a onetime concert pianist who switched to the popular field, wrote the music for Eddie Fisher's first picture, *Bundle of Joy*, making for a happy reunion of local talents in Hollywood.

And in pop music the town has really had a field day. Probably the most memorable hits were turned out by the late Joe Burke, whose tunes include "Tip Toe Through the Tulips" and "Painting the Clouds with Sunshine" (lyricist for these was the late Al Dubin, of Philadelphia), "Carolina Moon," Dancing with Tears in My Eyes," "For You," "Oh, How I Miss You Tonight" (lyrics by another localite, Mark Fisher), "Yearning," "A Little Bit Independent" and many others. More recently, young Bob Merrill has penned many big hits, including "Doggie in the Window" and "Candy and Cake." He also wrote the score for the Broadway musical, *New Girl in Town*.

Burke had the most big ones. But everybody, it seems, gets into the act in Philly. Everybody takes a stroll down Tin Pan Alley. A housewife, pretty former model Vicki Silvers, wrote "Learnin' the Blues" as her first try and it became a big record hit for Frank Sinatra. A former dentist named Clay Boland, who did many of the best scores for Mask and Wig, the University of Pennsylvania organization, wrote "Gypsy in My Soul." A former *Bulletin* police reporter named Bix Reichner wrote "Papa Loves Mambo" and many other novelty hits, A tailor named William Borrelli, Jr., wrote "Here in My Heart," the number which paved the way for Al Martino. Harold Karr, a dentist, and Matt Dubey, wrote the score for the latest Ethel Merman hit, *Happy Hunting*, which offered that catchy Hit Parade melody, "Mutual Admiration Society." And a long time ago Bobby Heath wrote "Pony Boy."

Jimmy Myers operated a little shoestring music publishing firm for years until he and Max Freedman wrote "Rock Around the Clock" for Bill Haley. Along with Haley, he has penned many of the hit rock 'n' roll tunes, the firm is no longer shoestring in nature at all, and Jimmy is smoking the best cigars.

Moe Jaffee, who co-operated on many of the Mask and Wig scores with Boland, is better known as the author of that oldie, "Collegiate." The late Jan Savitt, probably the top band leader from the town, wrote many of his orchestra's popular numbers. Al J. Neiburg did the lyrics for "Under a Blanket of Blue," "Confessin'," and many others. Incidentally, the music for "Confessin' " was the work of Negro song writer Ellis Reynolds, who had only that one hit. An engaging but improvident fellow, he died some years ago. His son, Howard, has been the pianist at Billy Krechmer's Jam Session.

Bobby Troup, whose first hit was "Daddy," hails from Lancaster (where his family has a music store) but he is a Penn alumnus who was a performing hit in Mask and Wig musicals. He now produces his smart numbers in Hollywood, where he is also known as a stylish pianist. Sammy Kaye made "Daddy" a hit and he first heard it at the old Embassy Club, where the house band was playing it as a favor to Troup. Another Penn graduate, onetime band leader Eddie De Lange, authored many hits of the thirties.

Many of the popular Western songs of our day are turned out by those city slickers, Jesse Rogers, Sally Starr and Rusty Keefer. Manning Sherwin, a Philadelphian who lived in England for many years, is best known for a number called "When Nightingales Sang in Berkeley Square." Other ASCAP gentlemen include Harry Link, better known as a publisher; the late Frank Capano; Johnny Fortis, who recently won the $500 Arcari Foundation Award for an original composition for accordion (the well-known accordionist Andy Arcari is a Philadelphian, too); Johnny Farrow;

Terry Gilkyson; Milton Kellem; Larry Fotine, another band leader; and Horace Gerlach.

Even Stuart Loucheim, head of the Academy of Music and a prominent businessman, got into the act. He authored that Rosemary Clooney hit of some years ago, "Mixed Emotions." And buried in a small Negro cemetery in Merion is a gentleman named James Bland, who wasn't a native but who lived in poverty and died in obscurity in Philadelphia. He was one of the great ones. You'll remember, for instance, a song entitled "Carry Me Back to Old Virginny."

And now, finally, about that other vital aspect of American life, that great sport of baseball. The onetime great New York Yankees' manager Joe McCarthy entered the Hall of Fame this year. McCarthy was born and raised in the Germantown section of our town. He was the twenty-eighth Philadelphia native or player or manager with a Quaker City team to be admitted to the Hall of Fame.

There are eighty-three members in all. And all of this was pointed out by Ed Pollock, sports editor of the *Bulletin*, in one of his columns after he had engaged in a little research following McCarthy's election to the baseball shrine.

"One in every three members," Pollock wrote, "played for and/or managed a Philadelphia club or was born in this city."

Not a bad showing. I'd go into detail, but you might think I was boasting.

Chapter XXI

But Everybody Can't Be Famous

ALL of the citizens, of course, can't be marquee names or juke-box favorites or book-jacket figures or familiar names in the Broadway colunms. There's an awful lot of coffee in Brazil, as the song says, and there are an awful lot of people in our town who never became famous. Most of them never will.

Certainly fame is never going to come to the late Waldo Maynard. Even if he were still around, he wouldn't have a chance for *Who's Who*. Waldo Maynard was a hunchbacked old man of eighty-four. Many people in the town knew him, without ever knowing his name. For a good many years he peddled his small wares in Olney and other sections of the town.

The simple facts of his life are these: He was born in Ashland, Massachusetts. As a young man he learned the weaving trade. He followed this trade until he became old, roving over our entire country. In the winter of 1938–39 his travels brought him to our town—an old man, a poor man, a beggar. That spring he moved into the Christian Settlement House and began to sell his small wares from house to house, establishing what he proudly called "my route." He lived at the settlement house until he was taken to the Philadelphia General Hospital, the charity hospital operated by the city fathers. He died there of cancer and he was buried by the settlement house. There was nobody to mourn his passing. He had no family, no known relatives.

Those are the basic facts of Waldo Maynard's life. But perhaps this should be added: In the last spring of his life, when his health failed rapidly and he had to go to the hospital, he was not worried about death. He did have a regret.

"Now," he told a casual friend, before he went into the hospital, "now I won't be able to cover my route and see all of my regular customers."

He had very little in life, in those last years. But Waldo Maynard never grew tired of living.

Ominsky won't make it. Sometimes I think he should. Ominsky staged a private rebellion.

First you have to understand. B. B. Ominsky is a pharmacist on Germantown Avenue. But these are times when you have to wind through lunch counters, hardware stands, and appliance shelves to get to the pills. A druggist has to be able to fry hot dogs and make hot chocolate quicker than prescriptions. He is a short-order cook with a title.

Well, for twenty-five years, a quarter of a century, Ominsky took it. He swallowed his daily ration of drugstore jokes.

"Whereja learn to maka ham sangwich?"

"You go to collitch for that, huh? Haw."

Day after day, through the years, Ominsky the pharmacist presided at the soda fountain. Then one day, some years ago, the climax arrived. A big medico walked in. Ominsky was sitting at his own fountain, eating one of his own hot dogs. The medico thumped him on the back and bellowed.

"Hey," the medico said, "you hear about the druggist gotta *cum laude* for his thesis 'Man's Best Friend Is the Tasty Hot Dog?' "

Seismographs must have quivered as Ominsky put down the hot dog. He made the medico's soda. The medico left. Ominsky began to think. He devoted forty-five minutes to a review and a forecast of Ominsky's career. He reached a decision. Cold, calm and deliberate, he went to work and roped off the eating oasis. Hungry customers walked in and were greeted by a quickly scrawled sign which informed them: FOUNTAIN CLOSED PERMANENTLY!

A few days later a big truck backed up to the store. It took out every luncheon department item from fountain and kitchen to toothpicks. Ominsky had jerked his last ice-cream soda. Ominsky was now filling prescriptions only. He was once more Ominsky the pharmacist. And who bought all the fountain stuff? Well, have an irony with your hot dog. The man who bought the stuff was Frank D. Green, grandson of the man who invented the ice-cream soda.

Johnny Brennan never made it. When he died he was pretty much a nobody. But the funeral parlor had to stay open a half hour beyond the set hour for the first time because so many people went out to say good-by to Johnny. And in the retrospect which is possible now, it seems to me that the fairly short and fairly happy life of my easygoing friend Johnny Brennan added up to one big fat irony.

Johnny was a ruddy, pug-faced little Irishman who rolled through the years with a grin on his face, a song in his heart, a persistent feeling that he could beat the horses and the sporting contests, a love for people and a zest for living. Thinking back now over the period of nearly sixteen years in which I knew him well, I can't remember a person he disliked, and I don't know anyone who didn't like Johnny. When he died he had nothing but friends.

Johnny's boyhood and young manhood, as the inspirational books always say, were tough. His father died at an early age and Johnny became the family provider. He never had any children of his own but he raised a whole family of brothers and sisters.

For a while he had a service station. He worked hard but there was a Depression on at the time. He lost the service station. Then he became a bookie and he had been doing well at that work for quite a few years when Uncle Sam called for his services. There was a war on at the time.

Nobody thought Johnny had a chance of becoming a soldier,

including Johnny. After all, he wasn't any youngster and he could hardly hear a thing in one ear. But they were taking the old ones and the married ones and sometimes the lame ones by that time. He made it. It was tough because he was old and out of shape. But he could take it pretty good and, before it was over, they had him in the gun crew of a 240-howitzer battalion, and there wasn't any cannon louder than that one.

When the war ended for us near Augsburg, Germany, they sent Johnny to a hospital and then they flew him back to this country to more hospitals to help his hearing. And therein was one of the ironies that helped to add up to the big fat one. All through the war he had stood guard regularly against the German troops. And right after the war, when we were nothing but occupation troops and the German soldiers didn't have guns, the doctors at the hospital said: "Why, this man shouldn't be standing guard. He can't hear."

So Johnny came marching home with a brand-new hearing aid (his walkie-talkie, he always called it) and the same old grin. He went back to being a bookie, but he bet too much himself, took too many chances without laying off, and was hit hard, so hard that he and his wife finally had to sell their home to pay off their debts.

It was time then to tuck away the grin for a while and Johnny did. One of his brothers, a younger brother, had built a successful new overhead door business. Johnny went into it. He worked hard. He learned it from the ground up, he learned all its varied operations—and this work wasn't the free and easy life he had known before. He really sweated out his . . . well, atonement.

Finally he earned and got his date with the Big Chance. He was to operated a newly constructed branch of the business in Canada. He was to be an executive, a boss, a man with responsibilities. He was happy and excited and earnest about it. He saw a whole new future with tremendous possibilities ahead for him. He and his wife gave up their apartment. They stored their furniture. She moved into a small temporary room while he went off to Canada to oversee some of the last-minute planning of operations.

A few weeks later he came back to Philadelphia to get his wife and his furniture, and to move to the new country, the new job, the new hope, the new life. He had only been back in town for a few days when he died suddenly of a heart attack. And there went the date, there went the Big Chance, there went everything. It seemed so ironic that after forty-seven years of living and sweat and toil and laughter, he died with most of his clothes in Canada, his furniture in storage, and his wife in a little room—leaving nothing much behind except a couple of hearing aids from Uncle Sam and a big gang of friends.

You may not have heard, Johnny. That first Derby you didn't bet on—Needles won it.

Billy Hey doesn't stand a ghost of a chance of making it. Tell you the kind of piano man Bill Hey is, or was, or never will be again. He always played real pretty. Made the tunes sound better than the notes that were written down for them, stuck in his own keyboard embroidery and it was good, it was in good taste.

And he could really back up a singer. Like with the notes, he made the singers sound better than the voices they were using. And they only had to run through a number once for Bill to know how they wanted it. Next time he'd be weaving nice patterns behind them, and they were always better singers out there in the spotlight because Bill was playing piano behind them in the dark. A lot of them could tell you that. Al Martino gave up the brick-laying and the first time he sang in public Bill was the guy at the piano. Al's done pretty well.

And Bill's helped a lot of others who were working the same musical bars and restaurants around town. Bob Manning, who sang on the Jackie Gleason show. Georgie Shaw. Dick Lee, who became big on the Sid Caesar show. Dolores Martel. And Sunny Gale long before she made it big with "Wheel of Fortune."

The wheel of fortune has spun real crazy for Bill in recent years. He was never a big name in show business. He was known and appreciated mostly by those in the business. He's the kind of entertainer who never held a full house or a straight flush. But he always had a pair, or maybe even three of a kind. He had a job. He liked his work. He loved the piano.

Now he's got an empty hand and he's out of the game and he

can't even write out an IOU against his future. His future? Let's look at it this way: If you're forty-two or so and you have a mother and yourself to take care of and all you know how to do is play the piano and now you can't play it because you're crippled, and you can't stand and you can't walk and you can't even hold a pencil in your hand, then you're Bill Hey.

Bill Hey is a tall, skinny guy with tired eyes planted deeply in a gaunt face. He comes from the Bridesburg section and he started to play the piano when he was seven, studying classical music. He had been playing it ever since—until everything went bad for Billy. For a brief time, in his younger days, he was a minor league ball player. And pretty good, too. "But I wasn't good enough," he says. "I wasn't big league material." And so he gave up baseball, which he also loved, and he stuck to the piano and, when he was only a kid of twenty-two, he was good enough to be the pianist with Mal Hallett's band, one of the top outfits of the thirties, one of the first big bands to really swing. Later he was with Al Donahue.

And then World War II came along and he was in the Army Medical Corps, where music wasn't as important as a lot of other things. When the war was over he came back home, and he settled down in his musical bars, just playing the piano real pretty, just backing up all of the singers—good, bad and indifferent—real pretty. Then, about five years ago, when everything was going along nice for Bill Hey, he "started to get funny little sensations in my knees.

"I didn't think too much about it at first. But the area of sensation started to get larger. Then I began to worry a bit. It was a strange thing, a real strange sensation.

"And I knew it wasn't good. I knew it could be something real bad."

In time, in too quick a time, Bill learned that he was a victim of multiple sclerosis. The sensations spread to his arms and his hands. He hasn't worked since.

"I keep hoping somebody might record one of the tunes I've written," he told me once. "I've written some good ones. That could help a lot.

"Or maybe I could do a disc jockey job. I can't stand or walk.

I have no control of my hands. But my brain still clicks and I have my eyesight and I have my speech.

"There ought to be something I can do."

The way Bill Hey felt at that time it didn't have to be a full house. Just a pair would keep him in the game. But they called off all the games for Bill Hey. He hasn't been able to do anything. A couple of years ago he got admitted to the Veterans Hospital in Fort Howard, Maryland, for treatment. Bill had high hopes, but the treatment didn't do any good. Bill came home. He still has hopes.

And I'll tell you the kind of town Philadelphia is. I ran a note in the column when Bill was admitted to the hospital at Fort Howard. Just a one-line note saying that piano man Bill Hey was there, and briefly summarizing his misfortune. It was just before Christmas time. Within a week Bill received more than six hundred cards wishing him well, wishing him the best. Many of them contained dollar bills, some of them carried five-dollar bills, although no money had been asked for at all. And a large number of the cards were from people who had never met Bill Hey, had never heard him play and didn't know anything about the real pretty music he could make.

I don't even know the name of another fellow who's never going to make it. But he deserves it. He is—or was—living proof that you don't have to be rich to have pride, that fame frequently taps the wrong guys on the shoulder and that a lot of unsung guys are greats of our time, too.

It was raining outside the night I heard this story. It was the kind of night for the story. A casual friend came up to me at the bar of the Latin Casino.

"How's everything?" he asked.

"All right," I said.

"Here's one you might be able to do something with," he said. "Or maybe it isn't anything. I don't know. It happened a few years ago now, so it isn't timely. And it wasn't anything sensational at all. But every once in a while I see some little old man walking along the street with an old briefcase, and I remember it . . ."

This is the story: There is in the town today—if he is still alive—

a little man in whom is embodied the inherent dignity of man. And if he is still walking the lonely streets, he will be carrying a briefcase. The satchel may not contain any important documents or papers. It may contain nothing at all, now. But it is a symbol. It is the little man's badge of honor.

He was an old man, our little man, and he had been a salesman for many years and he took pride in his job. A man working and earning money for a home, for a wife, for the kids, can walk the streets with head high. He does not bow for alms, nor plead for coins. He is fulfilling his own small destiny in life. But the years can catch up with a man's life and change it overnight. This man was old and younger men had come along, with more swiftness, more energy, more push—and more results, and he lost his job.

It is tough for an old man to find a new job. If you have ever been fifty or sixty, trying, you will know. And, in time, there was nothing the man could do except ask for unemployment compensation. His routine did not change, though. Even when he had gone on relief, he still got up at the same hour he always had. And he still left his home each morning with his briefcase. And he still walked the streets for the same hours he always had—except that now he had nothing to sell and was only buying a little pride for himself.

Then somebody reported him to the state. It was said that he must be a chiseler. He still went to work every day, it was said. And so the state sent an investigator to check on the little man.

When the investigator went into the house where the little man and his wife lived, he found that it was almost bare of furniture. They had been selling the furniture, quietly, piece by piece, to make ends meet.

"There are reports that you still have a job," the investigator said, "that you go to work every morning with your briefcase . . ."

The little man looked amazed, as though there was such an obvious explanation for this that it hardly required words.

"I didn't want the neighbors to know I was out of work," he said.

"And what about the briefcase?" the investigator asked.

The little man shook his head in puzzlement again. And finally, slowly, he explained. "I would feel lost without it," he said. The briefcase was the symbol of his dignity. He didn't say that, this little man who had been a salesman for many years and had lost his job and his part of the world—and didn't want the world to know.

"I would feel lost without it," he said. And then he closed the door quietly on the investigator from the state and his own life.

Chapter XXII

Some Older Citizens and Some Old Streets

EVERY schoolboy knows that the Liberty Bell is in Philadelphia.

Every schoolgirl knows that Betsy Ross—or so the legend goes—made the first American flag in our town.

It is common knowledge that Philadelphia is the home of Independence Hall, Carpenters' Hall, Congress Hall, the Betsy Ross House, Benjamin Franklin's grave, old Christ Church (founded in 1695 and designated a national shrine by Act of Congress), and a host of other buildings, places and institutions which are the very heart and foundation of our nation and its way of life.

It is plain fact that, historically, our town is by far the richest city in the country. All of this is taken for granted. The shrines have been written about and photographed and eulogized a million times. They have been visited by millions of people, family groups and solitary travelers swarming into the humid city during summer vacations year after year to make a kind of looking acquaintance with the spots where their liberty was born, their country created; and where great men, the founding fathers, unpretentious but farsighted and hopeful men, strolled on equally humid afternoons from Chestnut Street into the history books.

But there are two big things which impress me about Philadelphia's history that stand out above all the others. They are ever present, but they are perhaps unnoticed; and they should never be taken for granted because their value is too priceless. The first one is this: The noble legacies left by the two most famous Philadelphians, first citizen Benjamin Franklin and founder William Penn, are evident in virtually every phase of the city's life.

The spirit of the wise, witty and wonderful Ben Franklin hovers over the town like a guardian angel. He is everywhere, it seems, this amazing figure from the past, this most versatile man in the nation's life—writer, printer, publisher, scientist, inventor, educator, politician, diplomat, statesman, democrat, philosopher, businessman, lover, civic leader and citizen. He is there in the Benjamin Franklin Parkway, the Benjamin Franklin Bridge, the Benjamin Franklin High School, the Benjamin Franklin Hotel (with its happily named cocktail lounge, the Kite and Key Room), the unique Franklin Institute (in this perhaps most of all), the Poor Richard Club, the Franklin Inn and many other places.

On the anniversary of his birth they place wreaths on his grave in the Christ Church burial ground and they have ceremonies at Independence Hall and they wind up the traditional observance with a festive banquet at the Poor Richard Club, which makes a presentation of its Gold Medal of Achievement to some worthy citizen on the national scene for accomplishments in the Franklin fashion. But, more importantly, Franklin is somehow present in all of the town's progress, in its scientific interests and achievements, in its schools, in its libraries, in its medical advances, in its educational progress, in its cultural pursuits, in its many luncheon clubs, in its discussion groups, in its tolerance.

And it is in the town's tolerance that the legacy of Penn lives, too. Standing atop his perch on City Hall in the form of a 37-foot statue soaring 510 feet into the sky, Penn has no company except the pigeons which plague the pedestrians moving around the grubby architectural monstrosity which is the seat of the municipal government.

But his spirit, too, hovers over the people. His religious sect, the

Society of Friends, is comparatively small in numbers but strong in prestige and, more importantly, in influence. The Quakers remain an organization that gives more than lip service to belief in the freedom of the individual. Nowhere was that more emphatically illustrated than in the recent case of Mrs. Mary G. Knowles, the librarian at the Friends' Plymouth Meeting library.

Mrs. Knowles was convicted for contempt of Congress when she refused to answer questions about her past associations before the House Un-American Activities Committee. Despite pressure, no doubt, and risking popularity, undoubtedly, members of the committee in charge of the library, stouthearted Quakers one and all, promptly showed their faith and confidence in Mrs. Knowles by raising her salary from $3,200 to $3,400 a year.

Ben Franklin once remarked that "Without freedom of thought, there can be no such thing as wisdom . . ."

That $200 per annum may not have been an impressive figure. But it was an impressive salute to both Franklin and Penn.

And the second thing about Philadelphia history is this: It is not particularly, or it is not alone, the shrines themselves which enrich the atmosphere of our town. It is the feelings they produce, the feeling they can prompt of kinship between glorious past and troubled present. And it is the streets around them. The ghosts of the great walk all of the narrow, picturesque streets and alleys in the old section of our town—and that is why these streets and alleys are important, too.

They are important because Ben Franklin and the others, all of the founding fathers, once walked on them. History is in the air above them. History lies on their cobblestones. And if you take a stroll down toward the water front on a cold and quiet winter night or on an evening that arrives with summer calm, and walk over those old cobblestones, I assure you that you will not be walking alone. There is a very good chance that old Ben himself will be right beside you. And it's fine—and important—that he's still around.

That, too, is why a little street like Elfreth's Alley is important. Elfreth's Alley is the oldest continuously inhabited street in our country, and there is nothing else even remotely like it. It lies between Race and Arch streets and Front and Second streets. It is about six feet wide and it is, yes, paved with old cobblestones. Just as when it was laid out in the 1690s, there is a still a gutter in the middle of the street.

Most of the two-and three-story houses on the street are colonial English, and there are open-hearth ovens in most of them. Penn, Franklin, George Washington, Stephen Girard and many of the nation's founders visited friends in these same homes. Franklin, as a matter of fact, had a room in No. 108 Elfreth's Alley, which was built long before Ben had the room there—in 1694.

Mrs. Donald Willard, a direct descendant of Jeremiah Elfreth, the blacksmith for whom the street was named, still lives at No. 114. Jeremiah himself was at No. 137. Stephen Girard always stayed at No. 111 when he went down to meet the ships coming into the growing town from way across the sea.

No. 132 was the home of Philip Seng, and Philip Seng is very likely somebody you never heard of. Well, Mr. Seng was a silversmith. He made the inkstand used by the signers of the Declaration of Independence. A wooden water hydrant used by the early pioneers still stands in front of the Coach House, now a restaurant, at No. 135.

And down this street, down Elfreth's Alley, a girl named Betsy Griscom once skipped her way to the Rebecca Jones School in Bladen's Court. Betsy Griscom grew up and became Betsy Ross and made a flag and sewed her way into the history books and a nation's lore.

So it wasn't just any old street or alley that was threatened early in 1957 by a new expressway, the dastardly Delaware Expressway, trying to shove the past aside to make way for the speedy, rushing future. And the crisis was beautifully summed up and the threat placed in its proper cubbyhole by a *Bulletin* editorial writer, Frank McBride.

This is what McBride wrote in the Sunday *Bulletin* of January 20, 1957:

"Jeremiah Elfreth, the Blacksmith, came to Philadelphia in 1690. In the years following, his family acquired the houses in a little lane west of Front St. at the Cherry St. level. People got to calling it Elfreth's Alley.

"You can skip over the next 200 years. That's what Elfreth's Alley has done, paying little attention to yellow fever, the invention of the steel I-beam, or Frank Lloyd Wright. Hessian soldiers came and some went home again. So did the Boys in Blue and G.I. Joe.

"Elfreth's Alley stood still, and therein lies its claim to respect and survival. It is a little piece of the 18th century left living, not a waxworks museum piece like Williamsburg. The 31 houses are occupied by Philadelphians who choose to live there, not manned by models. All the residents and admirers of Elfreth's Alley really want is for it to continue.

"For those who fear that there's some truth in the phrase, 'You can't stop progress,' a new threat has risen to menace the Alley. It is a much more formidable threat than the British soldiers who roistered there in '77.

"The indomitable motor car is demanding new living space along the Delaware, and an Expressway along that river is virtually a sure thing. The latest and probably final plan weaves past a Benjamin Franklin Bridge abutment and the surfacing lines of the Market St.-Frankford high speed system. The easy way looks to be to bulldoze part of the Alley.

"It would be a pity to do it. The Delaware Expressway may be irresistible. Elfreth's Alley is irreplaceable and immovable. The point at which the subway comes to surface is neither.

"There must be enough engineering ingenuity available to fit all these components together. If the cost is greater, there are many Philadelphians who will consider it worth the price to hang on to a living fragment of the colonial past.

"A stainless steel plaque announcing that a certain ramp runs through what used to be called Elfreth's Alley would be a sad alternative."

Let's put it this way: Elfreth's Alley is not as important as the Liberty Bell or Independence Hall. But history is there, and it is a remarkable link with the past. And it is that way with a lot of the old streets in the old section of our town, not so plainly or so pointedly as is the case with Elfreth's Alley, but in the same way.

The atmosphere of history is all around us. It is in Independence Hall, surrounded mostly by grubby little buildings of commerce but clean and serene itself, with, as architectural critic Lewis Mumford once wrote, an "unassuming and intimate air" about it. It is in the daily ringing of the eight bells cast in England and hung in the tower of Christ Church in 1754, more than two centuries ago. It is in the churchyard there and the church's burial ground at Fifth and Arch streets, surrounded too by shabby, grimy little marts of merchandising. For in those two quiet, peaceful places in the heart of a noisy, bustling city lie the bodies of no less than seven of the men who signed the Declaration of Independence.

It is in a little street like Elfreth's Alley. And it is in a lot of streets that were walked by old men and young men who wrote their names courageously and built their new nation strongly.

You'll find those streets in Philadelphia.

Chapter XXIII

Billy Penn, Come See Your Town

PERCHED uncomfortably atop Philadelphia's pseudo-Renaissance City Hall stands a colossal bronze figure supposed to represent William Penn. His head sometimes lost in the low-lying clouds, his twenty-six-ton body clothed in un-Quakerly court dress, his feet, as it were, spurning the skullduggery that has too often gone on directly below him, he seems somehow unreal, unworldly, irrelevant.

"Of all our Founding Fathers, Penn is the least known to us. And yet, take him all in all, was he not the greatest of our colonial founders, the one who spoke and acted most forthrightly for the values we cherish—the values of fraternal equality, of political, civil, and religious liberty?"

That is the way Frederick B. Tolles, professor of Quaker history at Swarthmore College, began his review of Catherine Owens Peare's new biography *William Penn* in *The Saturday Review*.

The professor can write as well as well as he teaches.

Now, it's true that a heap of skullduggery has been perpetrated upon the citizenry from those offices along the gloomy City Hall corridors through the years. And it's true that Mr. Penn does seem a little unreal and unworldly up there in the midst of the Philadelphia skyscrapers. He never was a worldly fellow, as we know the type today. And he's been unreal for a long time. But irrelevant, no! Not even at this late date.

It strikes me that if he could step down from his perch up there with the pigeons and don some Quaker garb and take a stroll along the streets with the people, keeping a wary eye out for the heavy traffic from time to time, he would be proud of the big town he founded. It follows his teachings well. Democracy *is* at work here.

Tolerance, for the most part—and by most of the people—is almost taken for granted. The churches work unpretentiously together for the common cause, and the members of all of the many religious faiths and the people of all of the many nationalities work together casually and easily for the common good. They —again, for the most part and with most of the people—practice what is preached.

These are minor incidents that I present now, but perhaps they serve to make the point as well as more lofty discussion might. The members of the St. James Catholic Church at Thirty-eighth and Chestnut streets have no parking problems at all when they go to their house of worship. They haven't had for a couple of years now, not since the operator of the Atlantic service station and parking lot at Thirty-eighth and Walnut streets offered them the use of his lot for free on Sundays. The name of the man who operates that service station is Joe Klein.

Each week Christ Church puts out a little four-page printed bulletin called *The Beacon*. There was "A Word from the Rector" (who is the Reverend Ernest A. Harding) in the issue of February 24, 1957, which read thusly: "In the death of Mr. David Grossman, affectionately known to so many of us as 'Uncle Dave,' Christ Church has lost a valued friend and loyal supporter. He was one of the founders of the Old Christ Church Neighborhood Businessmen's Association and its Secretary from its inception. He has been a friend and confidant of Christ Church Rectors. He was a man who truly loved God and his fellowmen.

"Our deepest sympathy goes out to Mrs. Grossman and the family, and also to the Congregation Mikveh Israel where he was Treasurer."

There are Negroes in every phase of the city's life now, doing excellent jobs and causing not one whit of surprised comment or one slightly raised eyebrow. Where once the occupations available to the Negroes were almost solely those of the menial sort, where once they were principally servants in one fashion or another, they are now serving in a totally different sense.

Where once they were primarily elevator operators and trash men and garbage men and errand boys and street sweepers, they are now also teachers and lawyers and doctors and policeman and mailmen and trolley motormen and bus drivers and cabdrivers. And by the hundreds. And nobody thinks anything about it. They serve as well as their white brothers and often more courteously.

In May of 1957 the Philadelphia Teachers Association elected a Negro woman as president for the first time. She is Mrs. Edna Westberry Griffin, a grade school teacher for 34 years.

There are many good young policemen in the town, conscientious and hard-working, and many of the best of them are the young Negroes. These men, incidentally, along with the firemen, are a ridiculously low-paid group of citizens.

There are many Negroes on the sports teams of the colleges in the area, and in basketball and track particularly they have played key roles in bringing high athletic honors to the town. Villanova's champion track and field team includes Charley Jenkins, Olympic champion and one of the great quarter milers; outstanding high jumper Phil Reavis; and sensational sprinter George Sydnor. La Salle's Ira Davis broke the American record for the hop, step and jump and represented the United States on the Olympic team.

There have been many Negro players on the Temple basketball teams and they have helped immeasurably to carry the Owls to impressive court triumphs. When the brilliant and smartly coached quintet representing the school in the 1955–56 season finished third in the NCAA tournament, it was largely because of spectacular shot-maker Hal Lear and equally spectacular floor man Guy Rodgers. La Salle has had Jackie Moore and Alonzo Lewis on its basketball teams. And Villanova's future star may be Kenny Harrison, who just broke in during the 1956–57 season. Ed Bell, now a pro star with the Eagles, was a standout end for Penn.

In the high schools Negroes have virtually monopolized many of the athletic teams. Nobody has felt embarrassed about it. Nobody has noticed any change in the spirit or pride of those schools. Nobody has issued any shouts of horrors.

Billy Penn might not be able to believe his eyes at first but, after rubbing them perhaps, he would smile, I am sure, and think that it was all worth while, after all, threat of the H-bomb notwithstanding.

Now all of this is not to say that there is no bigotry or hate or intolerance in the town. This, of course, isn't any paradise on earth and there is some bigotry and some hate and some intolerance. But I think that these will be found here to a smaller extent, considering the circumstances, than in any other city in the country.

But there is in our town an increasing number of crimes, a tremendous surge in juvenile delinquency, and a startling rise in teen-age gang wars—in which Negroes are involved to an unfortunate and considerable extent—all reflective of a tragic national development since World War II.

The juvenile crime situation, to state it bluntly, is absolutely shocking. The official report of the Juvenile Aid Bureau for the year 1956 showed that 43.9 per cent of the eight major crimes (murder, rape, etc.) were committed by boys and girls under eighteen. In all, 10,270 youngsters (1,311 of them girls) were arrested, an increase of almost 2,000 over the previous year. The total complaints against teen-agers were 19,736, an increase of 17.2 per cent and juveniles were responsible for 29.2 per cent of all the arrests on charges of murder and non-negligent manslaughter. They accounted for 59.9 per cent of all automobile thefts.

There has been in recent years a really frightening rise in the number of teen-age thugs and hoodlums roaming through neighborhoods with pistols and switchblade knives, getting involved in brutal muggings, in holdups (many in daylight) and in robberies. And this steady rise in crimes committed by the young has been accompanied by an increasing savagery toward the hapless victims. Rowdyism and vandalism in the schools and on the trolleys and elevated trains has been equally alarming. The urge to destruction simply for the sake of destroying seems to have reached a new peak.

There are policemen in some of the schools now, of necessity. And it finally reached the point where special police guards were even assigned to the elevated trains, the subway surface cars, and other PTC lines in an effort to curb the growing vandalism and rowdyism. There are streets, too, that would astound the good Quaker if he were to walk through them. On one side there may be homes with fresh paint and neat lawns and clean pavements. And on the other side of the same street the houses may be shabby, with littered lawns and dirty pavements.

There is, only a few moments away from City Hall by car, a big section of the big town which has been called "the Jungle" by police. Roughly, very roughly, it lies between the two rivers and runs from Poplar Street on the south to Lehigh Avenue on the north. It is not all "jungle," I hasten to emphasize.

The boundary lines drawn by the police are too general, too expansive, and consequently they constitute an unfairness to thousands of good citizens who dwell within these borders and live out good lives in nice, clean and happy homes. They are decent and law-abiding and progressive, these citizens, and they take pride in their blocks and their neighborhoods and their efforts to improve them. And, quite justifiably, they bristle at the mention or suggestion that they are a part of "the Jungle."

Much of Philadelphia's best, its solid middle-class best, lies therein—in the heart of the city. But, unfortunately, therein also lies, through stretches of this territory, the heart of the city's crime. There are stretches and sections where Negro gangs run wild.

It is a part of the city where cramped living quarters and debris-littered stairways and booze-filled kitchens are the style, and crime is always in season. It is a part of the city where poverty rides in fancy new cars and television sets are more common than kitchen tables. It is block after block of rundown, broken-down homes, where the once neat brick row houses jutting on to the sidewalks have been turned into loose-living rooming quarters for many families in desolate and depressing circumstances, many of them newcomers to the town from the South.

There are 334,000 people in these nearly seven square miles between the rivers. The majority of them are good citizens. A minority has tried to make it bad for all. Here major crimes run to an

The new expressway

average of 612 a month—and there is always terror in the streets.

This is, as Charles Shaw, news director of the WCAU radio and television stations, once described it: "Philadelphia's shame and sorrow, Philadelphia's greatest menace, and Philadelphia's greatest challenge."

But for all of the violence in stretches of "the Jungle" and other stretches of town, there is a peaceful, friendly way of life in the other sections, in most sections, a good relationship between whites and Negroes. Block after block is occupied now by both white and Negro families in this town which named one of its municipally operated recreation centers after its greatest and most famous singer, Marian Anderson.

Almost always they live in harmony. They are striving for a common goal—to raise their families properly, correctly and as best they can. More and more the Negro adults are taking care of their homes as well as the whites. As a matter of fact, the Negroes, to whom the new home in the better neighborhood is a step up, an advancement, the symbol of the increased stature they have worked for and dreamed about, very frequently make their homes and their lawns neater. They have more pride in them.

White and Negro adults work together naturally and pleasantly in hundreds of business firms and factories. And the children play together. They play together as though there was no reason why they shouldn't, and it is good to watch them like that on the block and in the neighborhood where I live.

The town does right well by Billy Penn's tenets. It may not be an angel but it is always trying to wear its heart in the right place.

Chapter XXIV

It's a Big-Hearted Town

You can't pin down a happy time and you can't hold on to a fading love and you can't stop the clock for a youthful dream—and you can't really see the heart of Philadelphia on the brightest day of the year. But it's there, good friends, and it's a big thing.

It's there the same way Santa Claus comes down the chimneys of the world to paint delight in the eyes of innocent children. Its beat is loud and clear, and from time to time somebody does hear it that way, above all of the multitudinous sounds of a city's living.

Georgia Gerasimos crossed a continent and an ocean and came to this faraway city—and I think she heard it, one cold clear night in the winter of 1955, if only perhaps for an instant. Georgia Gerasimos was a young Greek girl, who was twenty-one when she came to our town. She was an orphan and lived in the little town of Coupena, in Greece. She was suffering from a heart ailment that needed the most skilled surgery.

One of Philadelphia's leading Greek-American citizens, who wanted to remain anonymous, heard about her case and made all of the arrangements for a four months' visa and her care in this country. And she came to Philadelphia, a lonely and frightened girl with no relatives to provide her with family love, to calm her fears; no friends to furnish her with companionship, to brighten her spirits; no English words to speak to those who were caring for her at the Hahnemann Hospital.

But there is a Greek program on radio station WJMJ, and one Sunday the girl's story was told on that program. Within half an hour men and women and girls of her own age were coming in to the hospital to see Georgia Gerasimos, whom they did not know at all. Each day brought more new friends. Greek priests stopped in. Flowers arrived at the hospital. Gifts were delivered daily. And Georgia Gerasimos found that she was not alone any more.

She discovered, too, that it is a very small world here in America, because this nation has had an invitation to the big world for many years. "Give me your tired, your poor . . . Send these, the homeless, the tempest tossed . . . I lift my lamp beside the golden door."

And thirty years before Georgia came to this country a woman named Mrs. Georgia Maltezos had passed through "the golden door" and she had been the flower woman in front of the Hahnemann Hospital ever since. And she had come to these shores, Georgia found, from the town of Coupena, in Sparta, Greece—and she had known Georgia's parents and her grandparents.

The heart surgery for Georgia was performed by Dr. Charles P. Bailey, whose brilliant and significant work in this field earned him the cover picture on *Time* magazine in March of 1957. It was completely successful. Georgia was taken to the Deborah Sanatorium in Brown's Mills, New Jersey, for her convalescent period.

Although she is a Greek Orthodox Catholic, all of the expenses of her hospitalization, surgery and convalescence were paid by the Deborah, a group of Jewish women, and other new friends she could not even identify.

She discovered that there are no barriers in languages—that there is one language above all, and it is the language for love and it is universal. She found that there are no differences at all in man's greatest religion, which is his love for his fellow man and his spirit of good will to all. And perhaps, on a cold clear night in the winter of 1955, a young Greek girl named Georgia Gerasimos may really have seen the heart of Philadelphia, if only for an instant.

Philadelphia is that kind of town, a bighearted town. If it is a city of homes and neighborhoods, if it is a city of churches, it is also a city of organizations, lodges, groups—each carrying out its charity and welfare programs with zeal and hearty good spirit. And the general theme of all of them is Brotherly Love.

The organizations represent all races, all religions, all creeds. And almost to a unit their contributions are spread around. Institutions of other races, other religions, other creeds, share in them.

The lives of many women outside their homes are built around "working for a charity." You have never lived in a small town until you have witnessed the induction of officers and heard the brief speeches at the annual affair of some women's organization from the stage of the night club which has been chosen as the scene of the festivities—and all of this in the *city* of Philadelphia.

The night clubs depend upon these affairs—and similar ones with the menfolks involved—for a substantial part of their dinner business, and fruit cups launch scores of lodges on a new round of helpful and worth-while activities each year.

They are amusing to watch, these affairs, the ladies bustling on to the stage in their best gowns and hamming it up a bit in the fleeting spotlight that comes their way so rarely. But they earn the right to feel important, for the purpose behind these affairs is serious and laudable—and there is nothing funny about it at all.

Aside from the organized, regular money-raising ventures or programs, the town responds swiftly to any sudden, spontaneous appeal. It delights in giving quickly to a family beset by unexpected trouble, a family that has been the victim of tragic misfortune, a boy who has lost a dog—the circumstances of which have been made familiar through newspapers. A home is burned down, a family is in dire need. The neighbors start collecting money. Community organizations join in. A boy loses his leg in an accident. His family is poor. The neighbors, the community, start to raise a fund for his future.

It happens dozens of times every year in Philly. Philadelphians love to help out, to make everything as good as they can for somebody who has had bad luck. I remember one story that illustrated this vividly. For if ever a boy discovered the way our town is, it was Larry Rosenthal.

When Larry Rosenthal died, he wasn't an important figure in the world. He was a sixteen-year-old Philadelphia boy. And when his story came to an end, it was a good story, the kind to warm the hearts of troubled people in a troubled age, because it was a reaffirmation of their own capacity for goodness. It was, you might say, a love story about a boy and a big town.

They gave the boy twenty-four hours to live when he was taken to Mt. Sinai Hospital (now the southern division of the Einstein Medical Center) with his spinal cord severed at the neck as the result of an automobile collision. Nobody knew Larry Rosenthal then except his folks and his friends in South Philadelphia High School and the neighbors around his home at 2214 South Eighth Street. He was fifteen. He played the clarinet in the high school band. He had a ready smile and a happy manner. He got a big kick out of life. That was about it.

He was just an average kid in the big town—except that he had to die. Then he quit being average and tried to make a fable out of fate and a myth out of medical knowledge and a stopwatch out of time, and how he did it nobody knew, not even the doctors. But thousands of people in the big town and around it cared, and they applauded and hoped for Larry as he fought for his life with a body that was helplessly crippled. In this day and age they courted a miracle.

And when he finally lapsed into a coma and could fight no longer, Larry was a great deal more than a kid clarinet player to thousands of people who, within a few weeks of time, had come to feel that they knew him very well. Larry never had a chance for life, except in his own heart.

He suffered his fatal injury on the way home from a high school basketball game at Penn's Palestra with a group of other band members. The doctors said twenty-four hours, but neither Larry nor his mother, Mrs. Walter Rosenthal, would believe them. From that night on, he couldn't move any part of his body. All he could do was lie in the hospital bed and smile and fight, first for hours and then days, and then weeks and then months.

The family—an average family in an average neighborhood—got private duty nurses for him day and night. Soon all of the savings and the Blue Cross money were gone. Then Max Leon, candy manufacturer and music patron, and his wife became interested. They helped out. So did Larry's music teacher, Michael Guerra. But that was only the beginning.

I heard the story of Larry's amazing fight for life and I told about it in my column, which was then appearing in the *Inquirer*. The big town heard about the story that way and it quickly proceeded to put its big heart on display, quietly and for the most part anonymously.

Here is what happened between the boy and the big town:

Hundreds of cards and letters arrived at his bedside. Scores of people went to the hospital to express their good wishes and their hopes to Larry personally. Boys and girls took up collections of money in their neighborhoods to help out on the expenses for Larry's family. Collections were taken up in many offices. Nearly $1,000 came to my desk to be sent on to the family, the amounts of the donations ranging from $1.00 to $50. Scores of donations were sent directly to the home or the hospital. Student nurses from the operating room sat with Larry hour after hour on their free time. They gave him a birthday party when he became sixteen. The Leons bought a television set for the room. Businessman Mark Abrahams arranged for special visitors to cheer up the boy.

The Phillies' ball players sent telegrams from New York—Larry was an ardent baseball fan—and the next day, when they returned home, three of the players visited him. Curt Simmons, Bob Miller and Eddie Waitkus, now retired from baseball, went to the hospital and presented Larry with autographed baseballs and bats from the club. That was in the afternoon.

That night—with Larry listening on the radio—Simmons pitched a three-hitter to win his first game of the season and Waitkus had four hits. The next afternoon Miller made the first major league start of his career and turned in a stouthearted winning performance.

Throughout his brave fight for life, the hospital treated Larry as a free patient. Dr. Henry A. Shenkin, the neurosurgeon in charge of his case, would take no fees. Numerous fund-raising affairs were held and others were being planned when the end came. "Everybody has been so wonderful," Mr. Rosenthal said one afternoon, talking about his boy. "You don't think it's possible in this day and age that so many people would care. We can hardly believe what has happened."

But it happened day after day. The messages of cheer, the good wishes, the help, the hopes, the visitors, the radio programs aimed at one boy reaching to the bedside from all of the stations. And each day and each night Larry, beyond hope and still with hope, gained new spirit in his fight. And he lay there smiling, sure that he would live, given strength and courage by what was happening, tremendously moved by the amazing number of people who cared about him.

But fate is not a fable, and medical knowledge is not a myth, and nobody can make a stopwatch out of time. It had to end sometime, only Larry wouldn't believe that and he lapsed into the coma after smiling through the television shows one night—and he never knew he was wrong.

"The last week was really the happiest week of his life," Mr. Rosenthal said, several days after the services for Larry.

That was the way the big town wanted it for the boy.

A mongrel dog named Terry ended a lot of lonely wandering one week end in our town. He rejoined his master way out in Racine, Wisconsin, writing happy ending to a story almost unbelievable in its unusual developments and involving a number of kind people in the town.

The biggest journey in Terry's life was made in style. He was flown from Philadelphia to his master on a United Airlines plane. And that trip ended the traveling which had begun eight months before for Terry, when he ran away from a place near Wilkes-Barre up in the coal regions—looking for his master—and somehow found his way to Philadelphia.

Ironically enough, it was a tragic incident, almost claiming Terry's life, which set the stage for the happy reunion of a man and his dog. Terry was struck by a car in Fairmount Park. He was with a small boy and another dog. They disappeared after the accident. But Miss Ethel B. Thaw and Mrs. Ann Winkler, who lived at 6308 Sherwood Road, happened along. Both of them love dogs and they stopped their car, put Terry on a blanket, and took him to the University of Pennsylvania's Veterinary Hospital.

The driver of the car which had hit the dog, Murray Harris, also loves them, and he insisted that Terry have the best of care at his expense. Terry was completely paralyzed on his right side, and it looked as though he would never be completely well again. This made Miss Thaw and Mrs. Winkler more anxious than ever to find his owner. Returning from the hospital, where they had made arrangements for Terry's care, they drove up and down streets near the accident scene looking for the boy. They couldn't find him.

Finally they made a telephone call to the Luzerne County courthouse in Wilkes-Barre, for the dog had a license from that county. They found that Terry belonged to Donald Foote, of Hunlock Creek, Pennsylvania, and they sent two telegrams and two special delivery letters to Foote. These were forwarded to Racine. The next night they received a call from Foote. He was extremely happy to hear that Terry was still alive and had been located.

"He must have talked two hundred dollars' worth," Miss Thaw told me later. And he asked that the dog be shipped to him, whether or not Terry was crippled for life.

"He's been too good a pal to forget him, now that I've found him again," Foote said. He explained that he had moved to Racine from Hunlock Creek eight months before, and had left Terry with a neighbor, who was to ship the dog to Wisconsin after his master was settled there. The dog had run away and had found his way to Philadelphia. Foote didn't know this, of course. All he had known was that Terry was lost and he would probably never see him again.

Miss Thaw and Mrs. Winkler offered to drive out to Wisconsin with Terry. Harris, the driver of the car, had to make a business trip to Chicago in the near future and volunteered to drive him that far.

"No, I don't want to wait," Foote said. "Ship him by plane as soon as he is well enough."

The doctors in our town did their job well, with the help of wonder drugs. Terry, they said, would be all right again. He would not be paralyzed on one side for life. He was coming along fine. And so Terry had the biggest thrill of his canine life. He was flown from Philadelphia to his master in Racine, Wisconsin—thanks to some Philadelphia people who know that any dog is just a little feller in a big tough world.

At the entrance to Fairmount Park there is a monument dedicated to Joan of Arc. One day a Philadelphian named J. W. Foster was passing the monument and he saw two boys about ten years old kneeling there, heads bowed in prayer. When they had finished the prayer, he went up to the boys and asked what they were doing.

"We stop and say a prayer to Saint Joan every time we pass the statue," one boy said. "To help his brother," he added, pointing to his little pal. "His brother's over in Korea."

The boys were kneeling in mud to say their prayer.

Chapter XXV

A Backward Glance at Long Ago

I FIRST saw Philadelphia on a warm summer day in 1930 when I came to the big city to register for the journalism course at Temple University.

I first lived in Philadelphia that fall. I had never been away from home. I had never lived anywhere except in my small town, Ford City, Pennsylvania, I was a lonesome, frightened boy in the big city. I knew so little about the big city that I asked a policeman where I could find the post office because I did not know that there were mailboxes on the corners into which letters could be dropped.

"There's a mailbox right across the street," the policeman said. "Just drop it in there."

He must have seen the hayseeds on my face. I found the mailbox, dropped the letter to my folks into it, and everything has turned out all right ever since then. I've had a good life in Philadelphia, and I thank the town.

I remember vividly, still, many things from my college days. I remember most warmly my close friends and classmates Natie Snyderman, son of a little confectionery store owner in West Philly; George Waller, son of a bank clerk in Lansdowne; and Phil Cameron, son of a coal miner in Shenandoah. I remember a lovely girl from California named Anne Sculley, who died so tragically young. And a girl from Ardmore named Ruth Kaplan. And later a girl from Aliquippa, Pennsylvania, named Jessie Gnarra.

I remember Mr. Wilson, an English teacher who meant so much, who drank beer with us and talked about writers and writing so well, and who died in an automobile accident one summer. I remember the wholly admirable gentleman who was Professor Henry E. Birdsong, the head of the journalism department, now retired and living in California. (I wrote home that his course was no lark. I thought it was a pretty clever line.)

I remember apples on the corner for lunch . . . Speedy's little confectionery on Broad Street above Montgomery Avenue, where I could read magazines for free if I didn't have money to buy them . . . The sepia shows at Nixon's Grand Theater . . . Standing on the curb and listening to the band music from Wagner's Ballroom right above the Nixon's Grand . . . Going to the Pearl Theater for the midnight Negro shows after cramming for exams.

I remember that great Negro runner, Eulace Peacock . . . My track coach, Ben Ogden . . . Dr. Negley K. Teeters in sociology (he's now the author of many books on crimonology) . . . Obie O'Brien shooting them in from the side uncannily for the Temple Owls in basketball (he's now a successful Catholic high school coach, has been for many years) . . . Swede Hansen on the football field . . . Pete Stevens on the same field (he's now the Temple grid coach) . . . Nelson Eddy singing at the Grace Baptist Temple on Sunday nights . . . The *Temple News* and the thrill of the first by-lines (on gymnastic meets, of all things) . . . The brothers of Sigma Pi.

I remember the Cathay Tea Gardens and the Little Rathskeller, where you could get by on comparatively little cash—and none of us had more than a little cash . . . The Parrish Cafe, my first Negro club—and the music was new and exciting . . . The Anchorage in the park, where we went for the late breakfast after the big dance . . . And the popular bands for the big dances were those of Mal Hallett, Isham Jones, and Ozzie Nelson, who had a girl vocalist named Harriet Hilliard singing with his outfit.

I remember the first tux, and I was uncomfortable in it then, and I refuse to wear one now.

I remember that the years, those good years, went by like mad . . .

It's a little book, and an old one now. But it still has a rich look about it. It still holds between its somewhat tattered covers something of the richness it brought to me many Christmas seasons ago. It is a rather frail little book, bound in leather, and with neat old type. George Gobel would say about it: "You just can't hardly get them kind no more." The title of the book is "A Christmas Carol," the first copy of it I ever had, the first one I ever read, and one that I have saved since 1924.

The book popped out from between some slim volumes of verse when I was going through my bookshelves the other night, picking out some old books to send to my nephews and niece back home. And it set some memories in motion. It placed me, a little sadly, in time.

"Merry Xmas From Mr. Reisgen, Dec. 25, 1924" is the inscription on the flyleaf of the little volume. It is written neatly, as figures might be handled by an accountant, which Mr. Ferd Reisgen was. He was chief accountant of the glass factory in my little home town, a short, methodical German who loved figures and good reading and precision and a brisk walk. He kept himself ramrod straight until the day he died, and morning, noon and night he strutted to and from his home and the office, swinging an umbrella like a weapon on days that threatened rain. And the people said, as they say of somebody in every town, that they could set their clocks by him.

A few years after 1924 I went to work for Mr. Reisgen as an office boy in the factory and that was the start of . . . well, of having a job. And seeing the name of Mr. Reisgen, I thought of another man and another job, because this man was always ramrod erect too, and he walked in the same way, had the same brisk manner and talked in much the same fashion.

His name was Mr. Craig, Bill Craig, and he was the managing editor of *The Evening Bulletin* the first day I met him. That was in 1936, in the midst of the Depression. I was working on a small-town daily in Monongahela City, Pennsylvania, and I wanted to get to the big city.

So I hitchhiked some 320 miles to see Mr. Craig about a job. I showed him some clippings of stories I had written for newspapers, I talked as well as I could, I expressed my great desire to work for the *Bulletin*. I was lucky. The *Bulletin* apparently needed a man. It was willing to take a chance. Mr. Craig said to go and see a man named Mr. Israel, Charlie Israel, the city editor—like Mr. Craig long retired now.

There was more talk with Mr. Israel and then he asked me how much I was making in Monongahela City—which, in case you don't know, is not far from Donora, where Stan Musial came from.

"Twenty a week," I said.

"Well," he said, "you won't be worth a darn bit more than that to us. Do you want to go to work for the *Bulletin*?"

I said that I did and I hitchhiked back to Mon City, proudly submitted my resignation, worked for two weeks and returned to Philadelphia. This time I didn't hitchhike either. I arrived by bus, traveling to a new life in the style to which a big city newspaperman with a lot of big dreams should be accustomed.

And that, I suppose, is when and how this book began.

Epilogue

"Hold It Down," the Editors Always Say

THIS, of course, is not all there is to say about Philadelphia. It is what I have happened to think of, sitting here at my desk in my "den," surrounded by a bookcase groaning with books, a basket of grapefruit and oranges sent from Florida by a friend, the accumulation of the week's newspapers, some of Muggsy's toys, a stack of pictures and etchings that can find no place on the walls at the moment, a vacuum cleaner, brooms and other odds and ends.

We call it my "den." Actually it is the pantry of an old house on Walnut Street, of which we occupy the first-floor apartment and are thereby fortunate indeed, since it gives us a front porch (I have always loved front porches and swings), a cellar (the handiest section of any house), and a backyard—a little backyard, but a backyard—which is for Muggsy. It, in fact, is why we moved here.

I have no doubt, unintentionally, neglected to mention many names and many places I would want to mention and should have mentioned. This I regret, and for this I apologize. But the editors are always telling you to "Hold it down. The story's running too long." And this has turned out to be a pretty long love letter to a big town.

Helen, my wife, just came in and asked how big a book it was going to be. "Well," I said, "I don't know how big the book will be, but I know what the big hope is—that I've got the town down. It's a pretty big and varied town to try to put between the pages of a book that is maybe an inch thick."

The discarded notes, the manuscript pages with the faulty starts, are piled high in the basket—and around it. But Lela will be here tomorrow morning to get rid of them. Lela Upshur, that is. A wonderful big Negro woman and a wonderful friend of ours and a good worker in her Baptist church, the Gibson Temple. She has been coming to our place once a week now since 1939. As I seem to have said before, we don't go in too much for quick changes in this town. We sort of like to go along in the old ways.

But it is time now to wind it up and send the copy along. It is time, too, to take Muggsy for his nightcap walk. He's ready, as always. And now, so am I. He's been very good throughout the book. I owe him a lot of walks. His dog friends throughout the neighborhood, down by the West Philly High School athletic field, on Sansom Street and Locust Street and Spruce Street and Chancellor Street, and everywhere else we stroll when the morning is bright with the newness of another day and when the night is tired with day's end . . .

Well, it could be that those dog friends have already begun to talk about Muggsy's old man. It could be that my reputation has suffered considerably. Somebody will have to tell them that I have been working on the book I have always wanted to write, about the big town in which I live.